THE
ALL-SEASONS
GARDEN

THE
ALL-SEASONS GARDEN

JOHN KELLY

VIKING

VIKING
Viking Penguin Inc., 40 West 23rd Street, New York, New York 10010, U.S.A.
Penguin Books Canada Limited, 2801 John Street, Markham, Ontario, Canada L3R 1B4

First published in 1987 by Viking Penguin Inc. in simultaneous hardcover and
paperback editions
Published simultaneously in Canada

The All-Seasons Garden was conceived, edited, and designed by
Frances Lincoln Limited, Apollo Works, 5 Charlton Kings Road, London NW5 2SB.

Library of Congress Cataloging in Publication Data
Kelly, John.
    The all-seasons garden.
    1. Landscape gardening.   2. Flower gardening.   I. Title.
SB473.K52   1987   635.9   86-40374
ISBN 0-670-81657-4

Printed in Hong Kong by Kwong Fat
Set in Goudy Old Style by Chambers Wallace Ltd, London

CONTENTS

FOREWORD

I HAVE THOUGHT FOR a long time that it is a great pity that, so often, gardeners seem to belong to one of two extreme kinds: the plantsmen and plantswomen and the garden-makers. If only they could be encouraged to share a common view of gardening! The problem seemed to me to be that the plantsmen and women regarded the plants themselves as all-important, while to the garden-maker it was only the overall picture of the garden that mattered.

When I was asked to write *The All-Seasons Garden*, I found that at last I had the chance to propose an outlook that would reconcile the two schools of thought – one that would lead plantsmen and women towards using their knowledge and eye for a plant to create a better kind of garden, and one that would turn the thoughts of the garden-maker in the direction of a deeper appreciation of the plants themselves.

Appreciation of all the qualities of particular plants, and how they can contribute to the interest of the garden at every moment of the year, is all-important. In this book, as well as discussing what can make a garden attractive all year round, how to create and plant it, and looking at it season by season, I have also talked a little about plant care and cultivation and have included a selective guide to some of the best plants for an all-seasons garden.

I am most grateful to Antony Paul for introducing me to Frances Lincoln and to Frances for suggesting the book to me. I have, too, been helped immeasurably by the editorial and design staff at Frances Lincoln Ltd, and especially by my editor, Sarah Mitchell, whose unfailing patience and charm have been an inspiration.

No gardening writer works in a vacuum. His ideas will be shaped over the years by conversations with other gardeners and they may never realise the contributions that they have made.

Among those whom I know to have made their views clear to me about the all-year-round value of plants are Geoff Hamilton, Roy Lancaster, Alan Mitchell, and Roy Elliott. There are sure to be others.

One's writings are shaped, too, by non-horticultural influences. Without Judy and Pat there would have been no book; Freda knew I had it in me to grow things before I did, and Nicky, my wife, is a constant source of encouragement, sound judgment, and help.

The All-Seasons Garden is dedicated to Lady Teresa Agnew who intrepidly allows me such free rein in her garden, and to her small grandson, Simon Morrison.

John M. Kelly

ABBOTSBURY, DORSET. 1987

INTRODUCTION

GARDENING IS THE ONE creative art that is accessible to all of us. To create a beautiful garden, you need a little space, a lot of interest, the desire to succeed and an instinct for beautiful things arranged in harmonious order – which will probably already be present as the stimulus of the desire to create a garden in the first place.

That the ordinary gardener (as opposed to the expert) will succeed is borne out by the millions of beautiful gardens that can be seen almost the whole world over. Unfortunately, far too many of them tend to have certain seasons in which they are at their peaks, while for the rest of the year they languish, waiting like larvae do for that short period of heady flight in the dazzling livery of fulfillment.

The part-time garden

The reasons for the part-time garden are many. Some are unavoidable, such as the types of climates in which it is possible to garden for only a brief period during the year. But even then, you can use the snowy trunks of birches and the varied tones and shapes of conifers to great effect in the cold, while agaves and cactuses contribute their strange contours to the hottest regions.

Gardening possesses a strong and a lasting allure. Often, it leads gardeners into the realms of monoculture and collecting. Monoculturists, whose gardens are packed with representatives of one genus, will never become all-seasons gardeners unless they rethink their position and return to the fold of balance and harmony. They and the collectors of plants – those growers of labels and card indices – use their spaces as one would a laboratory or a library. They are, and all gardeners must thank them for it, stockists and conservers of the plant riches of the world, but they are not makers of beautiful gardens.

Such people, however, are few; more usual are the great number of gardeners for whom unusual plant specimens are difficult to obtain. They find that they are limited to the range of plants stocked by the large garden centers, but the law of supply and demand dictates that such plants will inevitably be those that are grown for their flowers in the spring and summer – particularly the spring, for it is then that plants are mostly sold and they sell better if they are in flower. Even more numerous are those gardeners who have never really considered what their gardens could look like outside of the two great flowering seasons.

The all-seasons garden

One of the greatest delights of gardening is that once the full range of plants is known, you can choose a steady procession of trees, shrubs, bulbs and herbaceous plants that flower right through the year. When you discover that many genera of plants include members whose flowering times are a long way apart, you cease to think of crocuses, for example, as the Dutch ones that flower for such a short time in spring. It is possible to have crocuses of much more elegant natures in flower for many months. The ubiquitous Hardy Hybrid rhododendrons, with their short season of fat, blowsy trusses like frilly bathing caps, will give way to others, from which you can choose beauties to give daintiness and naturalness of flower from early spring to the end of summer. The herbaceous border will become a mixed one, where shrubs and roses give a permanent structure to a succession of flowering plants, heralded by the gold of *Euphorbia polychroma* and ended, very much later, by the rich red of *Schizostylis* and the blues and whites of *Agapanthus*.

There will be no lack of interest at any time of the year in this beautifully balanced scene. The strong upward-thrusting line of the large oak counterpoints the horizontal stresses of the fence, the stepping stones, and the spreading junipers. In winter, further vertical accents will appear as the bare stems of the magnolia and the background trees become prominent. The subtle positioning of the bergenias in the foreground, with their broad, rounded, evergreen leaves that are so distinct from everything else in the garden, ensures that they can be appreciated in every season.

Out-of-season qualities

The greater your knowledge of plants, the more you look for features other than flower. The flowering season of a plant is short and for the rest of the year the plant must make its growth and store its energy for the next reproductive bout. It is a poor occupier of garden space if it is merely a drab thing during this period – as, for example, is the popular *Philadelphus*, or mock orange, so loved for its bold, well-set white flowers and for its strongly aromatic scent in summer. After its brief blaze of beauty, it spends its winter as a shapeless bundle of twigs and the rest of the year displaying un-distinguished leaves of a torpid shade of green.

Compare this with the Mexican Orange Blossom, *Choisya ternata*. Again it is a shrub with white flowers and orangey scent, albeit flowering a trifle earlier, but here is a plant with all-seasons merit to a fine degree. Its evergreen leaves have a polished appearance all year round. The foliage is so dense that the branches cannot be seen; its freshness is a delight as much in the depth of winter as it is on a midsummer's day.

Where branch structure can be seen clearly, the all-seasons gardener should ensure that the plants are such that their woody parts are attractive. Instead of just having the brazen, overblown blossoms of the cherry 'Kanzan', you should grow instead *Prunus serrula*, whose flowers are a discreet, virginal white and whose frame, with its glossy mahogany skin, is de-liciously seductive at all times.

Look, also, to shape as a criterion of inclusion in the all-seasons garden. A tousle of twiggy tangles, such as the weigelas evolve, will not be of benefit. A small weeping tree, such as *Malus* 'Red Jade', can accompany the sentinellike shape of *Sorbus* 'Joseph Rock' in even the smallest garden, while shrubs with distinctive silhouettes in winter, such as *Viburnum plicatum* var. *tomentosum* 'Mariesii', whose branches echo those of *Cornus controversa* 'Variegata', will supplant the specimens that held sway because they looked smart for a week or two.

Large and small gardens

It is not only in larger gardens that the use of secondary characteristics of plants can be put to good effect. While the use of flowering succes-sion is inseparable from all-seasons gardening, it is not central to it. What is, though, is the idea that a garden is a finite space into which you can put an almost infinite variety of plants, but from this great variety you must select those that have something to offer at most, if not all, times of the year.

City gardens

Small gardens in large cities, for example, tend to be several degrees warmer in winter than

A lush all-seasons garden with a feeling of space has been created for a tiny yard a mere 7.3m/24ft long and 5m/17ft wide. In summer (right) there is an almost junglelike concentration of plants, overflowing from all sides, and vertical surfaces have been used magnificently. In spring (left) there is more of an atmosphere of urbane formality, in which the paving and clipped hedges are brightened by colorful spring flowers such as tulips, wallflowers and polyanthus. The permanent features – steps, curved paths surround-ing central beds, a pool, fountain and statue – provide a constantly interesting structure to the garden, and the background planting of evergreens, including Cupressus *species,* Choisya ternata, *and ivy, ensures year-round appeal.*

gardens in the surrounding countryside, and for this reason they are more congenial places for evergreens, which suffer in extreme cold. Gardeners whose busy city lives may mean that they come home just as the flowers are closing for the night can switch on their floodlights and admire the shapes, contours and shadows of fatsias, yuccas, phormiums and bergenias on their carpet of periwinkle and hart's-tongue fern – at any time of the year. They can inject the flower element into their designs by growing flowers in pots and putting them outside. Standard fuchsias will then display their pendent blooms well above the palmlike leaves of the fatsias, while the softer, more natural-looking of the pelargoniums will glow brightly above the deep green mat of periwinkle. This is a simple way of creating a small all-seasons garden.

Using perennials

In larger gardens, from the sort of size found in city suburbs upward, the emphasis must be on those plants that are hardy in the prevailing climate and that are permanent in nature. The all-seasons garden is not one that is remade each year: it is an organized entity that will grow and develop.

In such gardens, the largest population of plants will be of trees, shrubs and small shrubby (or partly shrubby) plants, while hardy perennial herbaceous plants will provide additional flower color and architectural shapes of a different type from that of their woody neighbors. To the greatest degree possible, every plant will add something to the all-seasons appeal of the garden, and those plants that do die down for the winter will have been chosen for their length of flowering, for flowering at unusual times of the year or for secondary characteristics of foliage or form.

While there is no reason whatever why annuals should not be grown in order to provide bright splashes of summer color, they do not come within our purview except as accessories, and fillers of gaps.

Planting designs

One of my particular dislikes (along with unnecessary pruning and superfluous feeding) is over-contrived planting designs, particularly those involving restrictive color-theme plantings. A garden based on one color – gold, for example – will look good in summer when much is in flower and in leaf. In winter, though, there will be yawning gaps where the coreopsis has retired below ground, the leaves have fallen from *Weigela* 'Looymansii Aurea', and *Robinia pseudoacacia* 'Frisia' stands thinly like an Elizabethan *grande dame* stripped of her finery. The same will happen with concentrations of blue, white or any other single color. Plants that are grown for only one desirable quality cannot make a garden with year-round appeal.

This does not mean that you cannot have individual color themes in a corner of the garden. Daffodils, *Philadelphus coronarius* 'Aureus', *Ilex* 'Golden King', *Gleditsia triacanthos* 'Sunburst' and *Phormium* 'Yellow Wave' would make a concentrated statement of gold all year round.

Garden features

Throughout the year, the walls, water features, paths and lawns are present as unvarying components of the general garden scene. As an all-seasons gardener, you should use many of these components as vehicles for growing plants. Indeed, you can use plants to complement such things as pergolas, walls, screens and water. What you must constantly bear in mind, though, is that such features must look pleasant and add interest to the garden at all times.

You should plan the siting of elevated structures and water features so that they fit in harmoniously with the contours of the land and with the envisaged heights and densities of your plantings, and also so that you can gain maximum pleasure from them in winter. This does not just mean that you should choose plants for their winter effect (pyracantha and cotoneaster berries on the walls; phormiums and the neat bamboo *Arundinaria nitida* by the water), it also means that you should place them where they can be enjoyed to the full from inside the house.

The juxtaposition of wall and porch has been enhanced here by an inspired all-seasons planting design. Plants that do double duty – that have flowers in one season, followed by shiny berries and winter evergreen leaves – are the cornerstones of the all-seasons garden, and the pyracantha is pre-eminent among them. Here, its deep green foliage is displayed to perfection against the stone wall, and it serves as both a herald and an echo of the changing seasonal picture framed by the porch; its red berries are as much a statement of autumn, and its flowers of summer, as the scene beyond.

The seasons

Although we refer to the seasons as if they were completely separate, nature knows no artificial divisions of the year. In subsequent chapters, several plants, such as snowdrops and *Hamamelis*, which are traditionally thought of as being winter-flowering, are discussed in spring, because spring, here, has its original, old meaning of 'the spring of the year' – describing the springing of new life from the ground. All-seasons gardeners, with a wide-angle view of the year, will rapidly discover that the traditional seasons blur one into another, and they will also find that their perception of what constitutes the seasons will start to change. Spring, for them, will start while other gardeners still have their noses deep in their winter reading, and the fruitfulness and color of autumn will last long after others have put away their tools, oiled their lawnmowers and said good-bye to their gardens for the year. While others forget the whole thing for some months, the greatly attenuated winter, for the all-seasons gardener, will still be a source of joy – not least because: "If winter comes, can spring be far behind?"

The contrast, richness and magical progress of the seasons is revealed in this garden, which has a simple but highly effective focal feature. In winter (left) the color of the bridge stands out against the surrounding whiteness, while its curved lines contrast with the stark branches of the distant trees. In summer (above) it forms a link between the greens of the trees and the bright summer colors of the flowers in the foreground, while it merges with and repeats the russets and reds of autumn (far left).

Planning the Garden

FORM & STRUCTURE

PLANNING A SUCCESSFUL all-seasons garden involves having a clear awareness of what the garden will look like in every season – not just in spring and summer, but in autumn and, especially, winter. The plants for the garden must be chosen with care and you must have a thorough knowledge and appreciation of those characteristics that make them look good all year round – their *form*. You should also be able to put these plants together harmoniously, and with your permanent garden features, such as walls, paths and hedges, to give the garden a solid *structure* and character, which will not only be attractive in its own right but serve as a backdrop to a year-round succession of flowers. Having flowers throughout the year is important in our definition of an all-seasons garden and you should choose plants that have long flowering seasons and use special techniques, such as gardening in depth (see p. 24), to extend the flowering season of your garden. However, a plant's flowers are not its most permanent characteristic, and what is especially important in an all-seasons context is its form.

Broadly speaking, form is what makes us like a plant *apart from its flowers*. Considering just how short-lived flowering is in most plants, it is just as well that so many of them have other characteristics that enhance our gardens and decorate the seasons when the plants are out of flower. Generally, form can be thought of as a combination of a plant's shape, size, habit – the arrangement of its stems and branches – and foliage.

Shape

The proper employment and deployment of plants with interesting shapes is vital to the making of a garden which will look good at all times of the year. Too many of one sort, or an overemphasis upon the grotesque, will spoil it.

Imagine a large garden in which there is nothing but rhododendrons. Out of the flowering season there will be interest present in the different leaf sizes and shapes, and to a small extent in variations of leaf color. The plants, too, will be of varying sizes. What will be uniform, on the other hand, will be their shapes. Every plant to be seen will have the silhouette of a parachute: round-headed canopies above stems arranged in fans. Now remove some of them from the scene and introduce a Cedar of Lebanon here, a fastigiate Hornbeam there, and put a weeping birch into one gap while the horizontal branches of an American Dogwood fill another. Already there is point and counterpoint; a sense of rudimentary harmony has been created merely through the use of shape.

I recently saw this harmony and contrast of shape in a small garden, in which the dominant accent was a golden Irish Yew (*Taxus baccata* 'Fastigiata Aureomarginata'), about 2m/6ft high and narrowly columnar. About its feet washed *Juniperus communis* 'Depressa Aurea', a widespreading patch of gold, while, for contrast of color, another juniper of spreading habit, *J. procumbens* 'Bonin Isles', but steel blue, lay at the front. It was a perfect example of how to use contrast of shape to good effect.

Size

Contrasts in sizes of plants are necessary for visual interest and harmony, and can also be used to make statements about their other qualities. A tall, columnar golden conifer with a smaller one nearby tacitly expresses something about golden-ness and columnar habit. Yet another dwarf one, at a good distance from the others yet placed so that all three can be seen at once, creates a theme. Taking things further, the theme can be picked up by something else that is

A magnificent all-seasons garden in which flowers play a very minor part, compared with form and foliage color. What little change that occurs as the seasons pass will only serve to reveal things now hidden. As Robinia pseudoacacia 'Frisia' loses its leaves, the blue foliage of the right-hand specimen of the pair of Picea pungens 'Moerheimii' will be the more clearly seen against the green of the tall Chamaecyparis lawsoniana. Golden foliage will continue, however, in the group of prostrate junipers in the foreground, among which are Juniperus × media 'Old Gold' and J. 'Pfizerana Aurea'. Their shape is in total contrast to the towering Cedar of Lebanon (Cedrus libani) which dominates the whole planting. Everywhere you look there are sharp contrasts of form, but the key-note is one of harmony, integration and unflagging interest.

Pyramidal   Columnar   Fastigiate   Weeping   Spreading

Shape
There is an extremely wide range of shapes among trees and shrubs. Some of the most common are shown here.

gold and then passed on to a large plant of a very different sort, thus creating a relationship within the garden that could not be made otherwise. Thus, *Chamaecyparis lawsoniana* 'Lanei' at one end of the garden could, by means of intermediates, be related to a totally different sort of golden foliaged tree, *Robinia pseudoacacia* 'Frisia', at the other. If the intermediate plants were of the same order of size as the principals, the result would be unrelated blobs of gold. By using smaller ones – *Thuja orientalis* 'Rheingold', *Erica carnea* 'Aurea' and *Philadelphus coronarius* 'Aureus' would be good examples – the eye is led to follow the theme.

Stems and branches
The color and character of stems and branches can be beautiful enough to make them objects of ornament in their own right, and they are important considerations in the all-seasons garden – especially where deciduous trees and shrubs are concerned, as it is these characteristics which will be displayed in winter.

There should be plenty of color in the all-seasons garden, and stem color in woody plants varies almost throughout the spectrum.

Indeed it is possible to find a plant to fit each color of the rainbow. For red there is *Acer palmatum* 'Senkaki'; for orange, *Myrtus apiculata*; for yellow, *Cornus stolonifera* 'Flaviramea'; for green, *Acer pensylvanicum*; for blue, *Salix irrorata*; for indigo, some forms of *Pinus bungeana*; and for violet there is *Acer negundo* var. *violaceum*.

Color of stems is what you should look for primarily, but there is also the matter of character. The trunk of the Maritime Pine, *Pinus pinaster*, is fairly evenly dark gray from a distance. Come up close to it, though, and you will see that it is made up of shiny, silvery plates of a more-or-less lozenge shape, separated by deep fissures which are nearly black. *Pinus radiata* has a dull bark which to many eyes is devoid of interest. Both are lovely tall pines but, all things being equal, choose the tree whose bark has that bit of character which will make you stop and look at it on the gloomiest winter day.

Barks that peel have a special attraction. The play of light on the bulk of the trunk or branch will give an effect which may be in total contrast to the same light viewed through the thin, papery sheets of bark as they curl away from the main body of the limb. This effect is there all the

RIGHT *The use of form is a vital aspect of all-seasons gardening, no matter how small your garden may be. In this tiny space the dramatic partnership of* Arundinaria murielae *(a noninvasive, neat bamboo) with the purple, sword-shaped leaves of* Phormium tenax *'Purpureum', will be equally evident in all the seasons. Its color is continued at ground level in* Ajuga reptans *'Atropurpurea', while the evergreen* Pieris japonica *'Variegata' completes a beautifully composed group. Ivies in the background and the broad leaves of* Fatsia japonica *help to create an all-year-round semitropical ambience.*

year round, and a tree such as *Betula albo-sinensis* var. *septentrionalis*, whose flaking bark is orange-pink, will go from bud to full leaf and from autumn tints to bare branches while the bark remains one of the most beautiful things in the whole garden.

Foliage

The same things, color and character, apply to foliage as a factor in the form of plants, although an extra dimensions is added in that they are important in nonwoody, herbaceous plants as well as in trees and shrubs.

Autumn color like that of the magnificent Japanese Maples hardly needs to be emphasized in its importance, although it should not be overstressed, because autumn is just one season, and the part of it which is full of the color of dying deciduous foliage is quite small. Autumn should not be thought of as exclusive to the deciduous plants, though, as some evergreens display bright leaf color among the other green leaves. *Stranvaesia davidiana*, when mature, turns some of its leaves bright red and they make a spectacular contrast with the fresh new, green ones that occupy the rest of the plant. Nor should the smaller herbaceous plants be forgotten. The creeping plumbago, *Ceratostigma plumbaginoides* is a case in point; its valiant reddening is so often overlooked by those who turn only to the larger inhabitants of the garden for autumn effect.

Plants that have striking foliage color – such as the red-purple of the Copper Beech or the purple forms of *Cotinus coggygria*, or the lemon gold of *Robinia pseudoacacia* – are important in the all-seasons garden, but should not be overdone. There are so many shades of green that yellow, red and purple should only be used to point up the distinctions between them. Gray is a different matter and can be used much more, especially when the greens shade down into the grays and the grays contain elements of silver. Variegated foliage is often best used to brighten dark corners, as many variegated plants will tolerate shade, and the evergreen ones, such as *Elaeagnus pungens* 'Maculata', strategically placed, are great antidotes to the winter gloom gardens can fall into.

Flower types

While form in a plant has to do with its out-of-flower qualities, flowers themselves have form as well. There is a wide spectrum of flower types, and the all-seasons gardener needs to take account of them when planning the garden.

In *Camellia*, for instance, there are single flowers with nine petals and fully double ones with a hundred or more; between the two is an almost infinite range of doubling. Furthermore, the sizes of the flowers can vary from about 2.5cm/1in wide to nearly 23cm/9in. It is all too easy to forget this when planting and to find that there is a severe clash of styles.

Not only its close neighbors but also the setting in general will determine whether a plant's flowers will look right. The fully double, quartered blooms of the Moss Roses fit very well into the mixed shrub border, especially when the roses are in groups. They need just a touch of formality and the very fact that a bed as such has been created introduces just the right note. Try to fit them into a glade in open woodland where there is little apparent structure in the planting (certainly no formal structure) and they will be completely out of place. On the other hand, the simple flowers of species roses will look as though they have always belonged in such a setting as, of course, they have.

In general, color clashes are fairly hard to achieve in the garden. Even such frowned-upon combinations as purple and gold can work well, but the way to create a clash is to mix the style of the flowers as well as the colors. The strong, sealing-wax scarlet of *Rosa moyesii* can be seen next to 'Arthur Hillier', another single flower with golden stamens but with a hint of blue in its red, but not alongside the Hybrid Tea 'Fragrant Cloud', whose red color does not clash, but its shape does.

ABOVE *Imaginatively chosen foliage can delight the eye for half the year at the least, while flowers endure for much shorter periods. Interesting leaf shape is as important as foliage color. Together they can create the stunning effect of this Japanese Maple, whose richly colored, deeply lobed leaves are here enhanced by an evergreen background of heath.*

ABOVE *The differing forms of flowers lend themselves to different uses and there can be very great variations even within a single species. The formal double white Camellia*

'Alba Plena' would not look at ease in an informal woodland setting among, say, species rhododendrons, while the single pink C. japonica would be ideal.

Evergreens

The use of plants with good form gives structure to the garden, and evergreens are preeminent among those that provide the most substance. The evergreen component of the planting in a garden can fairly easily be the most important single factor in determining its all-seasons appeal. Evergreens are, after all, wonderful all-seasons plants because they maintain their color and shape all the year round.

Evergreens used in planting designs need to be chosen with care and foresight. The last thing you want to create is a garden that is a uniform olive-green; what you should try to do is to vary the colors and to introduce an element of form by using a range of shapes that produce harmony and cohesion.

The evergreen colors that are available comprise a less restricted palette than may first appear – all thc shades of green, gold, blue and silver. The shapes are conical, globular, cylindrical, horizontal, or weeping, and the sizes are small, medium and large. Work out the permutations, and what a large amount of varied material you have at your command! The vast range of foliage types is, too, an almost inexhaustible fount. There is everything from the long, green needles of *Pinus radiata* to the great, broad paddles of *Rhododendron macabeanum*. Even down at the miniature level there is the neat, pincushion foliage of *Picea mariana* 'Nana' contrasting with the stubby, wider leaves of *Podocarpus nivalis*.

Think of a corner where a well-developed bay tree (*Laurus nobilis*) casts a shade. Its small leaves are of a light olive-green, wavy at the margins and densely packed. In front and slightly to the left is a young plant of *Rhododendron sinogrande* with shiny-topped leaves, 38cm/15in long and 15cm/6in wide, held almost horizontally so that their silvery undersides can be glimpsed. To the right is a rounded, compact bush of *Photinia* 'Red Robin', whose leaves are rhododendron-like and glossy, but are intermediate in size between those of the other two; it will, in the spring, have brightly russet-red new foliage. Just these three plants illustrate how form can be used to make a striking group – size, shape, habit and foliage characteristics all playing their parts.

The evergreen background

As well as giving structure and substance to the all-seasons garden, evergreens provide a good background setting for other plants and for flowers.

One of their most telling uses is in the preventing of 'silhouette' effects. When flowers are outlined against a bright sky they appear black and it is sometimes difficult to find a good vantage point from which they can be seen in their true colors, especially when they are well above eye level.

In my own garden, as every spring arrives, I find myself full of anticipation at seeing an 18m/60ft specimen of *Magnolia campbellii* in full flower. Its 20cm/8in rose-pink flowers bedeck the huge head of leafless branches in one of the most breathtaking sights in all gardening. That I am able to appreciate the flowers at all is only because they are seen against the deep green of the evergreen oak, *Quercus ilex*. Seen from a distance, the flowers appear to float in the air in front of the oaks; without them, the blooms would be lost to sight.

Not only flowers, but deciduous foliage in autumn color benefits from an evergreen background. The same evergreen oaks make a wonderful backdrop for the gold of the leaves of *Acer pensylvanicum*.

LEFT A *preponderance of evergreens provides constant all-seasons appeal. There is a balance of interesting shapes and subjects: the spiky phormiums; the small rounded conifers and the tall vertical ones; and a striking deciduous feature – the Japanese Maple. The mixture of summer- and winter-flowering heaths will form an ever-changing scene.*

ABOVE *Imaginative planting of evergreens can create all-seasons interest in the tiniest of areas. Slow-growing plants with interesting shapes, unusual forms and colored foliage combine with the old trough to give a sense of timelessness and an all-seasons garden in miniature.*

The evergreen–deciduous balance

In such ways a mixture of evergreen and deciduous shrubs and trees can be made to enhance the seasonal drama of the garden. Sometimes, though, you will want things to be seen as silhouettes, particularly deciduous trees with noble or interesting branch formation in winter. The English Oak (*Quercus robur*) is better with a background of sky, and so is the fastigiate Hornbeam (*Carpinus betulus* 'Fastigiata'), a tree whose teardrop shape is easily accommodated in small gardens. In a garden where there are many evergreens, such deciduous subjects should be grown in groups; just one standing out among evergreen foliage in winter looks as though it may be dead and not merely resting.

If space and climatic considerations allow, try to achieve a balance between evergreen and deciduous plants. Deciduous shrubs and trees enhance the garden by the variety of their appearance through the seasons. The plant that is subject to leaf-fall has opportunities to show off the colors which its foliage takes on before it dies and also to display any special features it may have in its bark or the disposition of its branches.

The ratio of evergreen to deciduous plants may, in some cases, be governed by climate. Many evergreens do not take kindly to climates with severe frosts. The reason for this lies in a critical truism which states that the amount of water lost by the leaves must never exceed that gained by the roots. This applies to all plants, naturally, but the deciduous ones solve the problem in winter by losing their leaves so that the roots do not have to try to extract water from frozen soil – an impossible task. As a rough guide, the softer and thinner the leaves of an evergreen, the less hardy to frost it will be; so the colder your garden, the fewer the kinds of evergreens that will be available to you. Similarly, once you are well into the warm-temperate zones, unless your garden is at some altitude, you will find it hard to grow many deciduous shrubs or trees.

23

Gardening in depth

A technique that illustrates the all-seasons approach is 'gardening in depth' – a term coined to describe the use of the vertical plane as well as the horizontal in order to extend the flowering season and the range of possibilities for year-round gardening.

Perhaps the simplest but by no means the best-known method of gardening upward is the use of trees and some of the larger shrubs as hosts, over and through which other, mainly climbing, plants may be encouraged to grow.

Clematis are almost always seen growing on walls, where they are supported on trellises and are pruned more or less heavily each year. When they are grown into other plants, pruning then becomes merely a matter of removing branches of the climber that are likely to produce flowers where they cannot be seen, thus directing the plant's energies to where they will be best spent. The point of the hard pruning of clematis is to induce them to flower down to the ground. Unpruned ones only flower at the ends of their branches, but this does not matter at all when they are grown into trees and shrubs.

This method of growing the genus also works on a small scale very well. Admittedly, the light pink or white of *Clematis montana* looks wonderful against the dark green of *Chamaecyparis lawsoniana* and is a sight not to be forgotten, but gardening in depth is effective at hedge level, too, where, for example, the silver-gray leaves of *Senecio greyi* can act as a foil for almost any strong colors, particularly in succession. The light, but bright blue of *C. alpina*, followed in turn by the deep lavender of *C.* 'Richard Pennell' and the wine color of *C.* 'Madame Julia Correvon', will make a worthy shrub into a wonderful source of flowers over a very long season.

Some care must be exercised when choosing the trees that are to act as hosts. Some evergreens resent the presence of intruders. It depends, too, on the guest plant. I have not seen a tree or a shrub damaged by the presence of a clematis, but the Kiwi Fruit, *Actinidia chinensis*, is too vigorous a vine for all but the most robust conifer. Wisterias are risky except where a tree has a fairly clean trunk (although it must have something to get hold of) but the advantage of growing them in this way is that they seem to flower very well without the summer pruning that is necessary when they grow on walls or pergolas.

Shrubs will display color for months when acting as hosts to climbers (left). Here, Clematis 'Jackmanii' scrambles through an informal hedge of Berberis thunbergii *'Atropurpurea'. Gray or silver foliage is an irresistible foil for white or pink flowers (right). Here, a white-flowered climbing rose creates an intriguing surprise among the gray, willowlike leaves of the weeping pear,* Pyrus salicifolia *'Pendula'. Clematis are among the most versatile of plants, and can be allowed to climb into trees (far right). The beautiful C. 'Marie Boisselot' has very large white petals.*

Climbing roses are perfect for gardening in depth, from the vast Himalayan musk roses that will wreathe the trunk of a 27m/90ft Scots Pine with white, to the deep rose-pink 'Zephyrine Drouhin' whose almost thornless stems can be threaded harmlessly through the branches of something like *Exochorda giraldi* and hang its double flowers from the large bush well after its host's single, white blooms have finished.

Growing one climber with another can be very rewarding. The leaves of *Schizophragma hydrangeoides* are not so very unlike those of *Lapageria rosea*. The flowers of the former are white, rather like those of a lacecap hydrangea, while the lapageria has large, bell-shaped blooms of a lovely, waxy, shining rose. They both require shade and shelter and can be grown in tandem in gardens that have reasonably mild climates. Just as the schizophragma loses its last flowers in late summer, the lapageria begins its display which will last well into the autumn, but sometimes they overlap with very startling results. Grow them over a shady archway in a wall and you will have utilized a difficult spot to perfection as well as having created interest and a prolongation of its flowering season.

Garden features

The structure of your garden is not only determined by the form and placement of your permanent plants; garden features are equally important, and they can provide interesting focal points or changes of level and layout. Walls, hedges and well-planted pergolas can even be used to mask off areas of the garden that are less interesting in winter, so that they cannot be seen from the house.

As an all-seasons gardener, you will obviously want to use the features of the garden to their greatest effect, both in their own right and as habitats for plants that will grace them in one way or another in all the seasons. A wall, a pergola, or even an existing tree are all good sites for gardening in depth.

Hedges

Hedges, like walls, have a profound influence on the character of a garden. They lend structure and interest to what might otherwise be flat, uninteresting sites, and their presence is important in winter when – acting as windbreaks – they not only make the garden a more comfortable place to be in but also contribute their differing shades of green (or even brown, as in the case of beech) and all their varying kinds of foliage to the winter scene.

Clipped hedges can sometimes look rather contrived but, used as hosts, they become vehicles for a succession of flowering. If the odd stem of the guest plant, such as clematis, becomes severed, it is not a tragedy and the overall effect will be much more colorful than unrelieved green. Hedges are much better windbreaks than walls because they filter the wind and, planted internally, they can protect a garden from the ravages of wind, as well as creating environments for plants that need shade or are a little tender. Internal hedges of *Rosa rugosa*, *Escallonia*, *Berberis darwinii*, *Fuchsia magellanica* and hydrangeas would almost make an all-seasons garden all by themselves.

Pergolas

Overhead structures, such as pergolas, that can be such an asset in achieving a vertical floral picture, should be deliberately placed in the garden for maximum impact. Indeed, a well-built pergola, especially if constructed on curves rather than straight lines, can so totally transform a dull, flat site that it very easily becomes the focal point of the whole garden and everything else will depend on it.

Plant it with roses, clematis, honeysuckle and jasmines, carefully chosen for a succession of flowering, and it will be a joy to walk along its cool length on a hot day when the air is full of scent from the plants.

A deciduous hedge continued over a garden gate makes a novel and attractive arch, providing changing seasonal interest and a splash of autumn color in an unexpected place. Garden gates are often overlooked as important features; a well-designed and maintained gate may well set the tone for the whole garden, and an all-seasons statement can be made at the very entrance in a simple yet effective way.

A fairly small garden that I know is one of those rare ones that has a stream running right across it and a wooden bridge. The owner has made a superstructure above the bridge from lightweight, curved steel tubing and all over it grows a very fine form of *Wisteria sinensis*. In full flower, the scent is a delight, especially as the flower trusses hang just at face level. What it needs for true all-seasons appeal is for other climbers to be planted and allowed to mix with the wisteria. Clematis varieties with successional flowering would be ideal, as their foliage is not incompatible in appearance with that of the wisteria, and hardy jasmines would carry on the scented ambience.

Lawns

The regularly mown lawn is an extremely pleasant feature in an all-seasons garden. It is green all the year round and it can, if kept well, emphasize the effects of the plants by the sheer contrast between its evenness and their variability. The edges of the lawn are perhaps its most important aspect. They really must be kept trimmed at all times of the year. Nothing shows up untidiness as frost does and ragged lawn edges can completely spoil some of the more intimate winter scenes.

The use of bulbs naturalized in grass is very much in the all-seasons ethos. The very best bulbs are daffodils and the scented Tazetta group of *Narcissus*, the majority of which will naturalize perfectly well. The grass may be closely mown between the drifts of flowers but the grass where they are growing should not be touched until seven weeks have passed since the last flowers have faded. Then it too may be mown and the whole area turned into lawn for the rest of the year.

Walls

A wall can be a great asset in an all-seasons garden. It enables you to grow a whole range of plants that can only be grown elsewhere with difficulty, such as Passion Flowers and *Clianthus*

Walls, pillars, steps and urns are features that give all-seasons interest, in their own right, and lend structure to the garden at all times, especially when herbaceous plants have died down. In this small and charming garden, stonework is used to provide changes of level, vertical and horizontal accents, and raised beds greatly increase opportunities for planting.

puniceus (the spectacularly beautiful, pinnate-leafed 'Lobster Claw', whose bunches of very large, brilliant scarlet flowers are unlike anything else). What it also does is to provide a ready-made vertical feature and the chance of a really warm sunny aspect in an otherwise cold garden. An ugly wall can quickly be hidden with beautiful plants, while one which is good to look at can be allowed to stand out as a feature on its own, particularly in winter when some of the plants that are growing on it have been pruned down. Clematis, for instance, can be grown through other plants on a wall which is best hidden and they can be left unpruned. On an attractive wall, they can be pruned for all-over flowering, in which case they will be down to short stems from late winter well into the spring.

Carpenteria californica is a good all-seasons plant for a wall. It has evergreen foliage and very beautiful, large, white flowers with golden stamens in midsummer. Grow it against a wall and plant *Ceanothus* 'Burkwoodii', rounded and dense and covered with dark blue flowers, in front of it, and in front of that again, the small shiny silver bushes of *Convolvulus cneorum* covered in large white trumpets. The wall will be a background, not just for a sheet of white, but for white-blue-white in ascending order in a vertical scene. What is more, the ceanothus will flower well into the autumn and the convolvulus, in a good year, will have been flowering since the middle of spring. Just as with growing things into trees, the proper use of a wall opens up ever more opportunities for making your garden into an all-seasons one.

Water

Water features in gardens often look dull except in late spring and summer. This is because water edge plants tend to die down in autumn, so the surrounding area is devoid of interest and there is nothing for the water to reflect in autumn and winter. However, a pond whose banks are planted with blue-stemmed willows, yellow- and red-barked dogwoods, and the

dramatic spearlike evergreen leaves of *Phormium tenax* will be an all-year round feature, not only because of the planting, but also because of the reflections in the water during every season.

The purely formal water feature, such as a small round pond with a fountain set in a patio or a flagged yard, can be a beautiful all-seasons feature in its own right. The play of water and its sound is always fascinating and creates a peaceful and reflective atmosphere which extends into the surrounding planted parts of the garden. Leave the fountain on as a freeze begins and see what fairy castles, crystal caves and grottos are created by the ice.

Evergreens, such as ivies and small conifers, ensure that the waterside planting will still be attractive when the herbaceous plants have died down. Structural interest is provided by the different levels of the ground surrounding the pond and the way in which the gentle curve of the pool edge contrasts with and highlights the solid, straight slabs of rock nearby and in the distance; these in turn complement the rounded shapes among the plants.

PLANNING PRINCIPLES

CREATING A GARDEN THAT will look good all year round is a matter of approach and of learning how to put into practice the principle that every part of the garden should have something in it that is attractive at every moment of the year. It does not matter how large or small your garden is: if your eye is fixed firmly on making everything that is in it a thing of beauty during all the seasons of the year, and on making sure that the garden as a whole is harmonious and beautiful, then the object will have been achieved.

Kinds of all-seasons garden

All-seasons gardening is a principle, which, once mastered, will lead you to apply it to whatever style of gardening you happen to have adopted. With the exception of gardens based on annual plants, there is no style that need not conform to the all-seasons approach. It can encompass the lush styles of gardening that make extensive use of richly planted borders and the spare, almost austere styles of Japanese gardens.

Borders

A purely herbaceous border will lack true all-seasons appeal, although judicious planting can ensure interest from spring to early winter. Herbaceous plants by definition die down in winter and, after they have been tidied up, there is little to see – often until late in the following spring. However, a more permanent sense of structure and an injection of interest throughout winter and in early spring can be provided by mixing herbaceous plants with shrubs and small trees, particularly evergreens. And, of course, a properly planned shrub border can be a marvel of interest all year round. A good way of illustrating the all-seasons approach is to consider planning such an all-seasons shrub border.

Planning a shrub border

A shrub border can demand considerable space, but the same planning principles should be applied to, and indeed many of the same shrubs can be used in, a small garden, as can be seen on page 37. You will do best if you start thinking about how the bed will look in winter and then work back through the seasons. It is fatal to start with spring; before you know it you will have filled up all the available space, and this is exactly what happens in a great many gardens and is why there are so few all-seasons gardens to be seen.

Start with winter and imagine the bed completely empty. For coral-red branchlets in winter there is nothing better than *Acer palmatum* 'Senkaki' and this small tree can be placed toward one end and about half way back. Toward the other end, say about one-third of the way along, the red bark theme can be continued with three plants of *Cornus alba* 'Sibirica', which will make bushes about 1m/3ft high of brilliant, bare, red stems. In complete contrast, *Betula jacquemontii* will display its almost pure white trunk at the back of the border, somewhere in the middle. Including some evergreens will not only create a balance but will also form a background against which the colors will glow. Behind the acer, plant *Chamaecyparis lawsoniana* 'Pembury Blue' – a conical conifer whose foliage is of a soft, steel-blue and which will reach a height of some 3m/10ft or so. To set off the cornus group, the golden foliage of *Thuja occidentalis* 'Rheingold', another conical conifer, will be in complete contrast to the blue one and will add visual interest.

Everything so far is vertical in its accent, so the fascinating structure of the tabulated horizontal branches of *Viburnum plicatum* var. *tomentosum* 'Mariesii' will introduce a balance.

A garden that abounds with good ideas. Acer griseum in the foreground is a small tree whose peeling, mahogany bark takes on wine-red tints in the low winter sunshine. It contrasts strongly with the gray foliage of the plants in the border beneath it, and the gray is echoed across the grass path, where there is a marked contrast of foliage color and form. This is a garden that is planned so that the house appears to be part of it – an effect attained by the use of climbers and of tall plants fairly near to the house. If there is one fault it is that the narrow grass path between the flowerbeds may become worn. A few flat stepping stones, set just below grass level, would emphasize the curves as well as obviating wear.

So much for winter. Look back, however, and you will see that the conifers will add to the scene at all times of the year, the acer will give lovely golden autumn color, the viburnum will flower in the middle or late spring, and the trunk of the birch will always be a focal point.

Turning now to autumn, if you have lime-free soil, you can plant *Enkianthus campanulatus*, a medium-sized shrub in the heath family, whose autumn color is in every possible shade of yellow and red. At the back of the border, place *Malus* 'Crittenden', whose bright scarlet crab apples will be present throughout the autumn and into the winter. You have introduced pale pink flowers for late spring with the malus, with sulfur-bronze ones on the enkianthus.

For the height of summer the front of the border will sport a drift of *Erica vagans* in groups of white, pink and red, while toward the back, but in front of the trees, the earliest of the blue hydrangeas, 'Vibraye', will reflect the sky in its mophead flowers. Near it, *Rosa rubiginosa* will produce its large, single, light pink flowers and cast its scent over the whole border. A different scent, that of pineapples, will drift down from the bright gold heads of flowers on the Pineapple Broom, *Cytisus battandieri*, grown as a freestanding specimen. These summer subjects will, too, contribute to other seasons; the heaths are evergreen and will make interesting bun shapes in winter, especially beautiful with frost on them. The leaves of the rose are fragrantly aromatic after the flowers have gone and its fruits are bright red and last well into the winter when they will counterpoint those of the crab apple. The silvery leaves of the broom are an adornment from spring to late autumn and often well into winter.

And so to spring. *Corylopsis sinensis* will eventually become a large shrub and should be placed at the back, where it will flower in early spring, drooping its numerous golden racemes before its leaves appear. Through it you can grow *Clematis* 'Henryi', which will show off its large, white flowers in late spring and again in

late summer, and 'The President' whose huge, blue-purple flowers will appear in early autumn. *Camellia × williamsii* 'C. M. Wilson' is a compact, rounded bush with large flowers like peonies in a soft pink. Its foliage will remain fresh and glossy all the year round, while the horizontal habit and single white flowers of *C. × williamsii* 'Francis Hanger' will both complement it and form a strong contrast.

Among the shrubs you can plant *Lilium regale* so that the huge flowers will come up into the summer sun while the bulbs are cool. They will follow the groups of *Primula pulverulenta* (deep rose-pink) and *P. bulleyana* (yellow) which will raise their 60cm/2ft stems with their whorls of flowers in the leafy glades in the bed. The primulas among the summer and autumn subjects

A seasonal comparison
Two slightly different views of a garden in which a delightful planting has been created, using mainly herbaceous plants. In summer (above) great use has been made of form, particularly in the making of strong, flowing groups of vertical accents to give life and movement to the scene. In autumn (right) seed heads, foliage and late flowers give structural and color interest. In order to achieve true year-round appeal, more use could have been made of shrubs and small trees, particularly evergreens. A framework of woody plants would eventually make this garden into a truly all-seasons one.

and the lilies among the spring ones will ensure that the whole border is colorful for a long time.

By working backward from winter you have created a border with constant interest and you have left out many of the plants that are so often planted for quick effect in spring. Had you thought forward from spring, it is likely that autumn and winter would have ended up looking rather sparse.

Japanese gardens
At the other end of the spectrum of garden styles, the principle of planning for winter is also important. There are several styles of gardening in Japan, and what they have in common is order,

harmony, and a genius for related plantings – and as much care is given to the appearance the garden will have in winter as to any other season. The poise of bare branches and their relationship to nearby evergreens or structures such as bridges is carefully considered. The viewing of colors against their backgrounds is planned and the use of the color that can be found in winter is raised to such a high art that a second glance is needed at a garden before the season can be determined with certainty. Although this type of garden is often relatively plantless, it is imbued with the spirit of the all-seasons garden. The raked gravel, the carefully placed stones and the overall harmony are there all of the year.

In this well-planned border, the shrubs, graded in height, provide great interest, even when very few flowers are to be seen. Green, variegated, gray-green and russet-gold foliage colors are carrying on fairly late in the year and have already been there for months. The old-fashioned rose still has a few late blooms. Prunus cerasifera 'Pissardii' in the background demonstrates how one carefully placed purple-leaved shrub or tree can have a profound effect on other, more distant, plants.

Harmony between house and garden is here achieved by using a Japanese-style spareness of design, in which many of the essential elements of all-seasons gardening are present in highly simplified form. The garden will be an almost unchanging scene of peace and tranquility throughout the year, but the passage of the seasons is marked by the changing color of the leaves of the vine climbing and trailing around the porch.

Small gardens

The tiny city garden, walled-in on all sides, may seem a poor candidate for year-round beauty. Plant it thickly with climbers, introduce bold foliage like that of *Fatsia japonica* 'Variegata' and yuccas, let brightly colored fuchsias glow against a dense evergreen background where green and variegated ivies cover the walls, set a small ornamental pond with a fountain in front of a tiny patio on which are pots of annual flowers, and you have an urban paradise upon which you can look with satisfaction at any time of the year. Using the all-seasons approach, the problem of filling a small garden with year-round interest can be solved in various ways, as the plans illustrated here show.

1. *Pyracantha coccinea* 'Lalandei'
2. *Acer palmatum* 'Dissectum Atropurpureum'
3. *Crocus speciosus*
4. *Geranium endressi* 'Wargrave Pink'
5. *Matthiola bicornis* and *Malcolmia maritima*
6. *Rosa brunonii*, *Clematis* 'The President', *C. montana* 'Elizabeth' and *C. alpina* 'Frances Rivis'
7. *Sarcococca humilis*
8. *Pyrus salicifolia* 'Pendula'
9. *Clematis* 'Ernest Markham' (up wall and into the *Pyrus*)
10. *Anenome japonica* 'White Queen'
11. *Enkianthus campanulatus*
12. *Fatsia japonica* 'Variegata'
13. *Hydrangea petiolaris*
14. *Cornus alba* 'Sibirica'
15. *Primula bulleyana*
16. *Hydrangea serrata* 'Intermedia'
17. *Rhamnus alaterna* 'Argenteovariegata'
18. *Jasminum officinale* 'Grandiflorum'
19. *Camellia* × *williamsii* 'Donation'
20. *Lamium* 'Chequers'
21. *Lavandula stoechas*
22. *Fuchsia* 'Tom Thumb'
23. Shallow stone bowl planted with crocus and small tulips for spring, in summer with light blue trailing lobelia, and with variegated ivy for winter
24. Spring and autumn bulbs (*Narcissus*, *Galanthus*, *Cyclamen*) among shrubs
25. Brick on edge capping to wall
26. Seat
27. Brick wall 1.8m/6ft high
28. Terracotta wall-mounted mask fountain
29. Brick edge matching lower level
30. Buff or gray pavers
31. Steps up
32. Low brick wall 0.5m/1½ft above lower paving level

Patio garden

Just a very few carefully chosen all-seasons shrubs, under-planted with early- and late-flowering bulbs, and with climbers planted on walls and garden structures, can provide constant color and interest. An imaginatively planted pergola gives further height and pleasant shade for the garden seat, and a wall-mounted fountain serves as a decorative feature all year round. Scent is also important in a city garden, and here it is provided winter and summer, with the sarcococca, jasmine, lavender and Night-Scented and Virginia stock.

LEFT *In a tiny, walled-in city garden the maximum use of light is paramount, as is the use of the walls as vehicles for plants. Here, the white walls achieve the former, while setting off to perfection the fresh foliage of the climbing plants. Whereas the wisteria makes a strong statement on its own (as well as hiding a drainpipe), the plants opposite are allowed to mingle and climb upon one another in order to produce a succession of flowering. The strong lines of the window, balcony and paving impose order on the whole scene. Color will come and go as the seasons change, but the basic structure of the garden and its permanent plants provide constant appeal.*

Shrub garden

The plants discussed in detail in the section on planning a shrub border (on pages 30-34) can also be used to fill a typical city garden with year-round appeal. Whether sitting on the terrace, or by the pool, or walking up the gracefully curved path, the garden will be seen to be bursting with interesting shape and color in every season.

1 *Lonicera periclymenum* 'Belgica' and *L.p.* 'Serotina' underplanted with *Geranium pratense* and small daffodils
2 *Phormium tenax* 'Yellow Wave'
3 *Clematis* 'Henryi'
4 *C.* 'The President'
5 *Corylopsis spicata*
6 *Primula pulverulenta* and *P. bulleyana* (among shrubs)
7 *Cytisus battandieri*
8 *Clematis* 'Jackmannii'
9 *Lilium regale* (among shrubs)
10 *Enkianthus campanulatus*
11 *Ceratostigma willmottianum*
12 *Malus* 'Crittenden'
13 *Hypericum × moseranum* 'Tricolor'
14 *Choisya ternata*
15 *Hedera helix* 'Goldheart' (growing up shed and on wall)
16 *Arundinaria nitida*
17 *Phormium tenax* 'Bronze Baby'
18 *Rosa* 'Cecile Brunner'
19 *Cornus alba* 'Sibirica'
20 *Viburnum plicatum* var. *tomentosum* 'Mariesii'
21 *Primula*
22 *Betula jacquemontii*
23 *Camellia × williamsii* 'C. M. Wilson'
24 *Camellia × williamsii* 'Francis Hanger'
25 *Pernettya mucronata* 'Alba'
26 *Philadelphus coronarius* 'Aureus'
27 *Hydrangea macrophylla* 'White Wave'
28 *Rosa* 'Golden Showers'
29 *Viburnum tinus* 'Eve Price'
30 *Chamaecyparis lawsoniana* 'Pembury Blue'
31 *Erica vagans*
32 *Rhamnus alaterna* 'Argenteovariegata'
33 *Acer palmatum* 'Senkaki'
34 Japanese Azalea 'Mother's Day'
35 *Hydrangea* 'Vibraye'
36 *Cistus × purpureus*
37 *Nandina domestica*
38 *Rosa rubiginosa*
39 *Choisya ternata*
40 Spring and autumn bulbs (among shrubs)
41 *Clematis montana*
42 *Polypodium vulgare*
43 *Cistus × corbariensis*
44 Raised pool
45 Brick wall lowers to 3 courses
46 Brick wall 6 courses high with stone capping for seat
47 Random stone paving
48 Table and chairs
49 Brick wall 1.5m/5ft high
50 Garden shed flat roof
51 Herringbone brick paving
52 Fence 1.5m/5ft high

A four-seasons garden

In the medium-sized garden shown on the right the emphasis, again, is on shrubs that look good all year round. Many, such as the *Pyracantha* and the *Mahonia*, are evergreen; all have good form as well as flowers or interesting foliage; and there are climbers – particularly various species of clematis. Here, also, there is room for a selection of trees. The larger trees give a background shape, the deciduous *Nyssa sylvatica* and *Acer cappadocicum* contrasting well in shape and foliage with the light evergreen conifers.

On the following pages, ideas for the all-seasons garden are discussed in spring, summer, autumn and winter. Each season is introduced by an artist's impression of the view of this garden, as seen from the terrace.

1 *Robinia pseudoacacia* 'Frisia'
2 *Prunus serrula*
3 *Pittosporum tenuifolium*
4 *Convolvulus cneorum*
5 *Nerine bowdenii*
6 *Clematis viticella* 'Minuet'
7 *Ceanothus* 'Blue Mound'
8 *Ceanothus* 'Puget Blue'
9 *Ceratostigma willmottianum*
10 *Cistus × skanbergii*
11 *Clematis montana* 'Rubens'
12 *Lavandula* 'Hidcote'
13 *Pyracantha coccinea* 'Lalandii'
14 *Rosa moyesii* 'Geranium'
15 *Cotinus* 'Velvet Cloak'
16 *Rosa* 'Souvenir de la Malmaison'
17 3 shrub roses: 'Mme Hardy', 'Louis Gimard' 'Honorine de Brabant'
18 *Hypericum* 'Hidcote'
19 *Cytisus battandieri*
20 *Nyssa sylvatica*
21 *Viburnum carlesii* 'Aurora'
22 *Chamaecyparis lawsoniana* 'Stewartii'
23 *Choisya ternata*
24 *Lonicera fragrantissima*
25 *Berberis darwinii*
26 *Acer cappadocicum*
27 *Clematis* 'Jackmanii Superba'
28 *Thuja plicata* 'Aurea'
29 *Clematis macropetala*
30 *Osmarea* 'Burkwoodii'
31 *Philadelphus coronarius* 'Aureus'
32 *Eucryphia* 'Nymansay'
33 *Viburnum plicatum* 'Mariesii'
34 *Pieris* 'Forest Flame'
35 *Camellia* 'Adolphe Audusson'
36 *Hamamelis mollis*
37 *Acer palmatum* 'Dissectum Atropurpureum'
38 Evergreen Azaleas
39 *Camellia japonica* 'Alba Plena'
40 *Rhododendron luteum*
41 *Rhamnus alaterna* 'Variegata'
42 *Rosa* 'Golden Showers'
43 *Callicarpa bodinieri* var. *giraldii*
44 *Mahonia japonica*
45 *Salvia* 'East Friesland'
46 Table and chairs
47 Stepping stones recessed for mowing
48 1.5m/5ft hedge
49 Bench seat
50 Brick wall 1.8m/6ft high
51 Statue

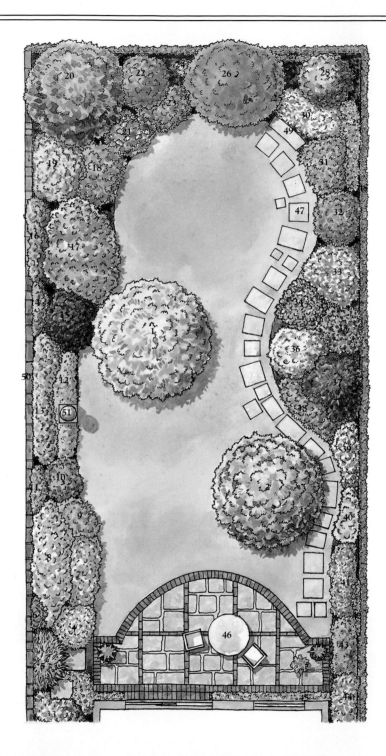

THE SEASONS

SPRING

In spring there is color everywhere, as the plants seem to race
to display their new-found foliage and bright, fresh flowers.

SPRING OCCUPIES A special place in our hearts, bringing as it does the romantic promise of warmth and blue skies. More important, from a gardening point of view, it brings with it a rise in soil temperature and therefore most new plant growth begins once again.

The gardening spring, however, starts well before this soil temperature rise occurs, in what is commonly thought of as late winter. The conditions that allow plant growth to get underway also induce the production of leaves on deciduous trees and hence the casting of shade. Plants of the woodland floor must make their appearance, flower and be well on the way to setting seed before this happens. These plants are not harbingers of spring, they are part of it.

Spring in perspective

Snowdrops are a perfect example of plants that seem to exemplify spring, but which, in fact, can flower in the garden for as long as five months. The genus *Galanthus*, to which they belong, includes several species that are so early flowering they might almost be called late. G. *nivalis* is the common snowdrop of the woodland and of the shade of the shrub border, but it is a very variable species, with subspecies flowering from autumn through to early winter and then picking up again in early spring. G. *caucasicus* has the longest flowering period of all the snowdrops, and its eight-week spread goes to emphasize that the division of the gardening year into seasons is, necessarily, rather arbitrary.

I do not think it is possible to have too many of these enchanting flowers. Set in drifts among trees, they make a bright carpet of white among the dark tones of the wintry wood, while in the small garden, their presence along the edges of the shrub border, or in among the shrubs themselves, gives a start to and prolongs that succession of flowers which the border will produce for the all-seasons gardener. Snowdrops are best moved while actually flowering, so of all plants they are perhaps the best for 'painting pictures'

with. They multiply rapidly, and you can lift flowering clumps and actually try them out in a new place. If you have a dark, bare spot that will be illuminated with daffodils later on, brighten it now with snowdrops – neither will resent the presence of the other.

Seasonal continuity

Just as snowdrops demonstrate that the traditional division of the seasons is different from the actual cycle of growth in the garden, a happy juxtaposition of plants can underline how the seasons sometimes overlap. A wonderful example of the seasons meeting each other involves two shrubs that have fine qualities for the all-seasons garden. *Viburnum betulifolium* has large corymbs of white flowers in early summer, followed by great masses of brilliant red berries. These berries persist right through the winter and on into the middle of spring when, if the two are planted next to each other, they will hang close to the flowers of the Purple-leafed Plum, *Prunus cerasifera* 'Pissardii'. Its flowers are pink in the bud, turning white, and they are borne in airy profusion before the young red foliage turns to a muted and very unobtrusive purple, which is a feature until the autumn. What more value for space could anybody ask for from just two plants, both of them hardy and both capable of growing on almost any soil?

RIGHT *The very essence of spring is displayed in this garden, whose planting produces a vibrant, though peaceful, atmosphere. There is color everywhere: blue from forget-me-nots (Myosotis) and Jacob's Ladder (Polemonium caeruleum), yellow from Alyssum* saxatile, *and azaleas add their touch of flame. The pond and the statue each provide a constant focus of interest as the colors and atmosphere change. It takes little imagination to visualize the daintiness that was here in winter, or the lushness that will overtake the garden in summer, before gold and flame return in autumn in the form of massed deciduous foliage.*

LEFT *A hybrid snowdrop,* Galanthus plicatus × nivalis, *appears brilliantly white against bare soil and rock in early spring.*

Spring on limy soil

The type of soil you have in your garden can have a profound effect on the variety of plants you can grow and this is, perhaps, more important in spring than in any other season. Spring is often regarded as the season of the lime-hating plants, and it is true that many of these plants are spring flowering, but the range of spring plants for the garden with limy soil is still extensive. Among them are some of the best plants for blurring the distinction between winter and spring – the Witch Hazels, *Hamamelis* spp. For scent they take some beating, and their odd flowers, which look like brightly colored spiders clinging to the naked branches, are like little else. The flowers vary from coppery crimson to bright yellow, and there are many varieties of the species *H. mollis* and *H. japonica* and of the cross between them, *H. × intermedia*. The usefulness of the Witch Hazels is by no means limited to early spring – their autumn color, usually a vivid flame red, is among the strongest and most flamboyant of all.

The hellebores do well on limy soils (as well as on acid). Both *Helleborus foetidus* and *H. orientalis* play a useful part in lightening a shady corner with fresh green foliage and bright flowers. *H. niger*, the Christmas Rose, is too well known to be emphasized, except to point out that two varieties are better than any others – *H. n.* 'Potters Wheel' and 'Trotters Form' – both of which have huge, white, disklike flowers close to the ground. They are, however, liable to soil-splash and they should be mulched with partly decayed leaves (see p. 132). Although their common name suggests otherwise, these plants usually flower in what the all-seasons gardener should think of as early spring.

Corylopsis is related to *Hamamelis*. All the members of the genus have more or less long, pendulous racemes of beautiful yellow flowers; they are borne on bare branches before the leaves are formed and are sweetly scented. They thrive on all soils, including limy, with the exception of *C. pauciflora*, which is a lime-hater. The owner of a smallish garden who wishes to follow the ideals of all-seasons gardening will probably decide to do without them, since they have little to offer after their early flowering, but they can claim a place in our design because of their early flowering and strong branch structure, which makes them a perfect vehicle for the later-flowering *Clematis*.

A planting design that puts to flight the idea that spring is the province of the lime-haters could have at its center a specimen of *Corylopsis sinensis*, bedecked with innumerable soft yellow catkins. Surrounding this would be *Photinia* 'Red Robin', which has bright red new leaves in a bold contrast of both color and form, and *Phormium tenax*, with strong, upright, saberlike leaves, bronzy-green in the spring sunlight. Just as the *Corylopsis* is past its best, the air will become heavily laden with the sweet scent of *Viburnum carlesii* 'Aurora' as it breaks into flower from its richly pink buds.

BELOW Hamamelis × intermedia 'Jelena' is a vigorous plant of spreading habit with large flowers that appear orange but are, in fact, yellow with a rich, coppery blush. The large, broad leaves turn orange, red and scarlet in autumn. They have a velvety texture that is pleasant in summer as well.

ABOVE *As well as fresh spring flowers, the Lenten Roses (*Helleborus orientalis *and its hybrids) have evergreen foliage that makes good year-round ground cover.*

Spring heaths

The great family of heaths and heathers is of great value at any time of the year, although gardeners with limy soil must confine themselves to the spring. The spring heaths are exquisite dwarf shrubs, which should be planted in drifts and savored for their season-bridging qualities.

It is a mistake to devote a bed or an area of the garden entirely to spring-flowering heaths, since it will be rather boring for most of the year. Do plant them in groups, but in positions where they will blend with other plants. In nature they occur in clumps rather than in continuous carpets, and they will look right if you repeat this pattern in your garden. They need plenty of sun and air, so do not place them on the shady side of taller plants. Rather, plant them on the sunny extremities of borders and in beds where their foliage can play a useful role in shading the roots of plants that require such shade.

The spring-flowering heaths belong to the genus *Erica* (the vast majority of late summer heathers are *Calluna*). *E. carnea*, of which there are about 30 really good varieties, is a fine plant, which should be planted in groups of about seven in order to avoid 'spottiness'. Unlike other heaths, which are moorland plants, *E. carnea* is from the mountains and is, therefore, appropriate near or on a rock garden. In nature, this plant is often the scaffold around which large black ants build their homes, and the resulting mounds of earth help the stems to root and keep the plant compact. You can achieve the same result in cultivation by dibbling a peaty mixture among the stems, thereby avoiding lankiness and a tendency to die out.

Of the varieties of *E. carnea*, 'Winter Beauty', a rose-pink form, is another season-blurring plant that flowers in late winter. Between this one and some others, including 'Atrorubra', the season for the species can be, and often is, as long as six months. Foliage should never be overlooked either. 'Vivelli' has a neat habit and its rounded humps take on a deep bronze hue in

RIGHT *With evergreen foliage ranging from deep bronze to pure gold and with plants varying from compact to robust, the many forms of* Erica carnea *provide never-ending interest, while a wide choice of varieties will give flowers for six months. The main flowering season, however, is in early spring. Lime-tolerant, and looking right in a rocky or a moorland setting, this versatile, weed-suppressing species of total hardiness is one of the best and most useful for gardens. The cultivar shown here is 'Pirbright Rose'.*

winter, setting off the rich carmine flowers to perfection.

Erica carnea is not the only species that will tolerate lime. Similar in this respect is the much taller *E. mediterranea*, which flowers after the *carnea* varieties are ending. It grows to about 1.2m/4ft and it can be planted singly among the drifts of its smaller cousins, 'Alba' is about the tallest variety, while 'W. T. Rackliff' is popular for its masses of white flowers.

Magnolias

Of all the trees and shrubs, magnolias are the most redolent of spring. Their flowers are magnificent, and they have a simple nobility of bearing and foliage that makes them graceful inhabitants of the garden at all times of the year. While some are definite lime-haters, many are a great deal more tolerant of it than most people realize. Most magnolias that wane and die over a period of some years do so because their roots have been damaged at an early stage in their lives. For long-term success with magnolias, you need to plant them with great care (and a lot of peat) and they must never suffer from drought.

The flowers of the larger ones are best seen against a background of dark green foliage, especially the pink ones of M. × *loebneri* 'Leonard Messel'. This can be grown in a fairly small garden, but the perfect magnolia for the smallest garden is M. *stellata*. Some thought does need to be given to the consorts of this lovely small shrub, which only attains medium size after a long span of years. Its starry white flowers against the glossy green foliage of camellias are a delight. It will stand a lot of lime and on such soil something suggestive of a woodland environment goes best with it – photinias are good, as are viburnums. M. *stellata* is a plant of considerable year-round appeal. Its silvery-furry buds are formed late in the year and adorn the leafless shrub throughout the winter months.

Magnolia × *soulangiana* has those upright, chalice-shaped flowers in white with varying degrees of purple blushing at their bases. It is, in time, a medium-sized tree, and then its countless blossoms borne on naked branches make a breathtaking sight. Later, the large, paddle-shaped leaves lend something of a tropical air to the garden, and neighboring plants should carry on this idea, while conserving the woodland spirit of the genus. The larger-leaved rhododendrons, the pinnate foliage of *Robinia* and the American Dogwoods will all provide the right atmosphere as well as taking up flowering where the magnolias left off.

Dogwoods

The American Dogwoods are tolerant of slightly limy soil, but do not do well when the soil is very alkaline. Some cannot be beaten for their beauty of flower and their autumn color is extremely good indeed.

The Eastern Dogwood is *Cornus florida*. In mid-spring each tiny cluster of totally insignificant flowers is surrounded by four heart-shaped, white bracts, like large apple blossoms. Indeed, a pink form is called 'Apple Blossom'. An even deeper pink one is *C.f.* var. *rubra*; 'Cherokee Chief' and 'Cherokee Princess' are deep pink and white, respectively. 'Rainbow' has foliage that is irregularly but effectively marked with red, pink, purple, cream and green.

C. nuttallii is the Western Dogwood. It has six to eight pointed white bracts and its foliage usually turns gold in autumn (as opposed to the red in *C. florida*). It needs the sun of its native home to keep it in good health, otherwise it tends to die suddenly in maturity. Its hybrids with its Eastern cousin, though, are a different matter. Take the four white bracts of *C. florida* and multiply them up to the number held by *C. nuttallii*, let them remain heart-shaped and not pointed and increase their size by almost half. Add a dash of hybrid vigor and you have one of the most spectacular small trees of the garden – *Cornus* 'Eddies White Wonder'. Its great billowing clouds of fully rounded bracts are the perfect complement to the bright colors of spring, and it is hardy, tough and quick growing.

A spring comparison
A well-planned garden, planted to look lush and green in
spring (below), need not lose its attraction in winter (right).
The bold shapes of the conifers and the inviting curve
of the evergreen hedge are central to the structure of the garden
in all seasons, while the starker elegance of winter gives way
to the fullness of the spring scene

Spring on acid soil

If your garden is highly charged with lime, then camellias are not for you. But a soil that hovers around the neutral mark is acceptable, provided plenty of acid, humusy material is incorporated.

Camellias are among the great spring spectacles, but the genus *Camellia*, like *Galanthus*, knows no artificial divisions between seasons. *Camellia reticulata* flowers early in the spring and it is sumptuously spectacular. You do not need to worry about placing it near plants with less showy blooms, since it will probably be over before they start. *C. reticulata* is not the hardiest of camellias, but its hybrids and some clones are much tougher than many of the varieties. 'Captain Rawes', thought for many years to be the species, is perhaps the hardiest form of *C. reticulata* and it will stand short frosts down to 14°F/−10°C in woodland-type conditions especially when its wood has had a good chance to ripen during the previous summer.

Where just a few camellias are being grown, it is better if they are planted in a small grove rather than being dotted about individually. A solitary camellia never looks as though it belongs. Their other neighbors should be well chosen. Plants that are not of the woodland look fine nearby, as long as they are of markedly different stature and require different amounts of sun. A low ceanothus, such as 'Blue Mound', in the sunny edge of the border in front looks well. Also, try some of the lime-hating Californian irises, such as the purple *Iris tenax* or the yellow *I. innominata*, fairly close to, but not among, them, and you will bring a little subtle color after the camellia flowers have gone. The true colleagues of the camellias are rhododendrons, but choose later-flowering ones that will carry on where the camellias leave off.

Many new camellia forms and hybrids have been raised recently and some of them are among the most beautiful flowers in cultivation. *Camellia japonica* has so many varieties that it is just about impossible to count them, and this camellia is a plant for the front rank of the all-seasons garden. Its foliage never loses its bright, polished look nor its amazing capacity for reflecting the sun. The play of light on *Camellia japonica* is something you will never tire of.

Rhododendrons

The flowering period of a rhododendron is short, but you have to live with its foliage for the whole year. The Hardy Hybrids are dull, repetitious and uninteresting, especially when out of flower. Species Hybrids, on the other hand, are usually much better, retaining the natural elegance of the species.

Camellia × williamsii is the name collectively given to hybrids between C. japonica and C. saluenensis. Plants of this cross are generally very hardy and their buds are frost-resistant, their foliage is attractive at all times of the year and has a naturalness that lends elegance. 'Donation' is probably unsurpassed among these hybrids. Its large informally double flowers are of a soft pink with darker veining on the petals and its flowering season is very long. The plant is perfectly capable of covering itself with flowers so that it looks like a pink pillar.

Foliage should be your first consideration in choosing rhododendrons, then size. A large garden can accommodate a selection of plants ranging in size from large shrubs to small trees; a medium-size garden can have a selection of rhododendrons that never exceed medium-shrub dimensions; while a really small garden can contain a range of dwarfs.

The largest-leaved of all are *R. macabeanum* (yellow flowers), *sinogrande* (white) and *falconeri* (yellow). These are tall shrubs or small trees with huge, broad leaves like green leather, and they are truly majestic when emerging from surrounding bamboos or casting their shade over a carpet of hardy geraniums and early primulas. They do need proper protection from wind but they can be hardy enough when such protection is given.

Camellias and Species Hybrids go well together. The rhododendrons will, in general, flower after the camellias and their two types of foliage are sufficiently different to make a nice contrast and yet they share an indefinable affinity. There is no better underplanting for these plants than hardy ferns mixed with candelabra primulas or even polyanthus – the atmosphere of the woodland floor can be readily transferred to the garden.

Rhododendron thomsonii flowers in the middle of spring, but its attractions are by no means confined to its flowers. Its smooth, plum-colored bark is lovely all the year round, and the rounded leaves are very distinctive. The clusters of seed pods, with persistent, apple-green calyxes are pretty and long-lasting. It is an example of the superiority of the species and Species Hybrids for all-seasons appeal.

Among the many Species Hybrids that are suitable for the medium-sized garden are several with true all-seasons qualities. *R. campylocarpum* has neat, ovate, apple-green leaves with bell-shaped yellow flowers. It is a hardy shrub and its many good hybrids include 'Lady Bessborough' and 'Crest'.

Dwarf rhododendrons are not plants of the woodland, but of the open moor. They need a moist, peaty soil and they will tolerate a lot of sun. The owner of a small garden can enjoy the genus in miniature by using them and they are perfectly at home among heaths. Very few have uninteresting foliage, while some, such as *R. yakushimanum*, might almost be called foliage plants if it were not for their lovely flowers. There is a long succession of flowering and they can play an important part in extending the year-round interest of the garden.

Azaleas

Azaleas are plants of the late spring on lime-free soil. They cannot be grown at all on soils that are limy, no matter what devices and excavations are made in an attempt to do so. They represent such a valuable addition to the spring palette, though, that they are worth growing in raised beds or even in large tubs, provided that these are filled with a lime-free potting mix.

Azaleas are, in fact, rhododendrons, and there are two main types – the evergreen (or Japanese) azaleas and the deciduous azaleas. Both are sufficiently distinct from what we normally think of as rhododendrons for us to consider them as separate groups of plants.

Japanese azaleas are small shrubs and their use in the garden is similar to that of heaths and heathers in that they are best grown more in the sun than in the shade and in groups of one color. While their flowering season is short, they are evergreen and their foliage is always tidily pleasing, and they make bright hummocks of green around and among taller subjects. Their color range is wide, from pure white through many shades of pink, red, vermilion, lilac, purple

and a color that is almost blue. On a large scale, they can be seen at their best as borders to long lawns or as if a multicolored lace ribbon had been laid along the edges of a woody area. In smaller gardens the same principles can apply. A tall variegated holly with a group of pink azaleas ('Blaauws Pink' or 'Mothers Day', for example) will make an enchanting contrast of light and dark and, later on, a contrast between the variegation of the holly and the green of the azaleas.

The perfect all-seasons plant

There are few plants that captivate people completely when they first see them. One of these is the perfect companion for rhododendrons and for all plants that enjoy an acid soil and light shade. *Pieris* is a small genus of evergreens whose foliage is good throughout the year, but one – *Pieris* 'Forest Flame' – is a plant of such outstanding quality that it seems almost too good to be true.

Its story starts in autumn, when panicles of flower buds are formed. These remain to decorate the plant right through the winter before developing in the late spring into clusters of nodding, white, pitcher-shaped blooms. At about the same time, new growths of the most amazing, brilliant red appear. This color slowly turns to shrimp-pink, then to white, before gradually becoming suffused with a lovely green.

Pieris 'Forest Flame' is just about the nearest thing you can get for the open garden to the effect of 'Poinsettia'. The new growths are susceptible to frosts. Nevertheless they will grow again if damaged in this way. Dappled shade allows sunlight to enhance its dramatic colors, while protecting it from scorch.

Deciduous azaleas are very different. The range of colors includes white and pinks, but with the addition of yellow and orange. The reds tend to be more intense and to have a deep, fiery quality – as does the autumn foliage color, which is among the most glowing and dazzling of all plants. Deciduous azaleas grow reasonably tall, and after many years they can attain a height of about 2.5m/8ft, but they are still best planted in groups, if space permits.

Where there is room for only one example of deciduous azalea in your garden, try a group of, say, three plants of *Rhododendron luteum*. This golden-flowered species is the yellow, scented azalea and its perfume is far superior to that of the honeysuckle.

Once again, their strong colors look marvelous against a background of green, composed of plants that flower after the azaleas – *Ceanothus*, *Escallonia* and *Hydrangea*, for example.

There is a Japanese air about this garden that owes much to strong accents, the use of water, and the early visualization of the eventually mature picture. Although the azaleas have a short flowering season, there is much to come (including magnificent autumn color) and the water will reflect the changes of the seasons.

Spring bulbs

Bulbs, of course, regard spring as their playtime. The all-seasons garden should have plenty of them, but do not plant them in beds of bulbs alone, since there will be little of interest from early summer onward. You can, however, create a succession of flowers in one place by planting bulbs in layers (see p. 130).

Use bulbs as components of the garden picture and of the mix of plants at ground level; for this reason the highly bred florist's varieties, beautiful as they may be, are out of place in the all-seasons garden. The valuable contribution to the spring garden of snowdrops (*Galanthus*) has already been mentioned (see p. 42).

Narcissi and daffodils

The shorter narcissi and daffodils look very effective indeed in drifts. You can achieve this informal look by throwing bulbs down and planting them where they fall. This produces a natural effect, just as if they had been spread by seed, and avoids any tendency to 'block' planting. There are many varieties, of which those with the blood of *Narcissus poeticus* and *N. pseudonarcissus* are easily grown and always look right. A great and deserved favorite small narcissus is 'Tete a Tete', which is a pure yellow and only about 20cm/8in high. It often has two flowers on a stem. Away from severe frosts you can grow the neat, bunch-headed Tazetta group of *Narcissus*. They look magnificent under trees, and varieties can be had in white, yellow or bicolor and are all scented.

Crocuses

C. chrysanthus, with over 20 excellent varieties, is an early-flowering species that combines elegance and restraint without loss of color. *C. sieberi* 'Bowles White' is one of the most lovely of all crocuses, while *C. minimus* has an effective combination of buff and purple with scarlet stigmata and flowers four to six weeks after *C. chrysanthus*.

Cyclamen

These plants are indispensable components of the spring bulb scene. The forms of *C. orbiculatum* var. *coum* are bone hardy, very early flowering and they have flowers that are reminiscent of tiny ships' propellers. They range from white through various pinks and down to deep purple-red. Clustered around the trunks of trees, they make an extremely

cheerful sight. Much later in spring, *C. repandum*, the Ivy-leaved Cyclamen, whose pink or crimson flowers are richly scented, appears in rather more sunlit places. In colder gardens, plant cyclamen so they are shaded from direct winter sun.

Erythroniums

Reflexed flowers, such as are found in the cyclamen, occur in another bulb genus for the spring garden – *Erythronium*. *E. dens-canis* is the only European species and it will grow happily in any good soil and in sun or shade. It is typically mauve, but there are white forms. The American erythroniums prefer shade and are happiest among shrubs or under trees. *E. tuolumnense* has large, golden flowers and it is easy to grow, as is *E. oregonum* 'White Beauty'.

Tulips

For the all-seasons garden, the best examples are the 'Water Lily' tulips of the *greigii* and *kauffmanniana* series. The former are long-lasting flowers with short, strong stems and they come in bright colors. They are best placed away from the more informal parts of the garden and they often look good planted near the house – perhaps by a patio, for example. Their leaves are prettily marked with streaks of maroon or purple-brown, and these stay as an ornamental feature after the flowers have gone. *T. kaufmanniana* varieties are earlier flowering than most tulips, they have extremely short stems and, where crosses have been made with *T. greigii*, the leaves will be handsomely marked.

Cyclamen orbiculatum *var.* coum *(right) can be used to great effect by being grown beneath early spring-flowering trees, such as Hamamelis mollis, whose flowers will appear at the same time. Here it creates a mossy, patchwork quilt together with* Eranthis hyemalis *which, in spite of being called the 'Winter Aconite', displays its golden flowers in early spring.*

Erythronium 'Pagoda' *(below left) is a hybrid of E.* tuolumnense *with even larger flowers and taller stems.* Erythronium 'White Beauty' *(below) will tolerate conditions that are a little drier than those required by other species.*

Narcissus 'Mount Hood' *(far left) is one of the best and most vigorous white daffodils. It has a slight gold flush when first open.* Chionodoxa luciliae *(left), a dwarf blue-flowered spring bulb flowering among a wonderful pattern of roots.* Cyclamen *species follow in summer and autumn, providing a miniature all-seasons garden.*

Scent in spring

Scent is at its most captivating in spring, and it is a good idea to have scented plants near the house, along favorite garden walks or near garden seating and natural resting, or pausing, places.

Many viburnums are among the very best of scented shrubs for all kinds of good soil. *Viburnum carlesii* has white flowers, which are pink in the bud and produce a scent similar to that of daphne, only stronger. Its foliage is rather stiff, but the downy, gray-green leaves have character and turn a pleasant color in autumn. It has two popular varieties: 'Diana' and the stronger-scented 'Aurora', both of which have red buds opening to pink flowers. *Viburnum* × *burkwoodii* is white flowered. It is a taller-growing shrub with shiny leaves, and it has the bonus of flowering over a long period from late winter to late spring. Another fragrant viburnum is *V.* × *carlcephalum*, which resembles *V. carlesii* except that the flowers are much larger. It is winter hardy and has brilliant autumn foliage.

Osmanthus delavayi is a small shrub with neat, rounded leaves, white flowers and an extremely sweet perfume. *Osmarea* 'Burkwoodii' is taller than the osmanthus and it presents its white flowers at head height.

Choisya ternata is an evergreen shrub, whose glossy, trifoliolate leaves are a delight at all times of the year. If you gently crush a leaf it gives off a sweet, aromatic scent, while the white flowers have the scent of orange blossom. It is surprisingly hardy for a Mexican shrub and it will stand a lot of frost. It is a good-tempered plant that flowers over a long period of the spring and into the summer.

Choisya is seen at its best if clipped and in a larger garden it makes a fine hedge, especially inside the garden along the edge of a path. As a freestanding shrub it tends to sprawl and its branches are prone to breaking. It is one of the few shrubs that really does need to be pruned to keep it showing its great all-seasons assets.

Climbers

One of the glories of late spring are wisterias. The most dramatic by far is *Wisteria floribunda* 'Macrobotrys'. There is no more exciting plant for a pergola, arch or the superstructure of a wooden bridge. The huge, dangling racemes of fragrant, blue-lilac flowers can be as long as 1.2m/4ft, and a well-developed plant will carry masses of them. The foliage is pretty and you can use it as a foil for other plants that flower later in the season.

Should you want to grow wisteria up and through a tree, then one of the forms of Chinese Wisteria, *W. sinensis*, is just the thing. The racemes are 30cm/12in long (borne before the leaves appear), the flowers are scented and even the seed pods are prettily silvery. Colors vary from lilac to deep purple and there is also a white variety called 'Alba'. It is a memorable sight to see this and 'Black Dragon', a dark purple, double variety, growing together up a sturdy tree. Unfortunately, wisterias are seen far too seldom growing in this way, especially since no extra garden space is taken up by them and they are an adornment to trees that might otherwise be unexciting at this time of year.

Clematis

Clematis is one of the most popular genera of garden plants, and yet it is underused. The large-flowered hybrids are seen everywhere during the summer, usually on walls and trellises, while *C. montana* is used in the same way in spring. They do, indeed, look well in such situations. In nature, however, clematis grows up trees and over rocks and bushes. In our desire to use plants to produce flowers in all seasons, we should think of employing the genus in its natural way so as to give shrubs and trees a second garlanding of flowers. Moreover, if the right varieties are chosen it is possible to have clematis in flower the whole year round.

In nature, *C. alpina* scrambles over rocks although it is very much at home over a shrub

The concept of gardening in depth is spectacularly exemplified by this spring scene, in which Wisteria sinensis *nobly festoons a group of trees. Climbers grown in this way look very natural – no wisteria, carefully trained, tied in, and annually pruned for flower production has half the majesty or sheer presence of one growing, as nature intended, on host trees. The long, gracefully pendent racemes of scented flowers need no stone wall or other artificial background; set against dark green foliage, their delicate coloring is seen to the greatest advantage. The rhododendron in the urn in the foreground echoes the tone of the wisteria, and adds to the majesty of this beautifully planted garden. Other climbers – clematis, campsis and roses – coexist with the wisterias and promise months of beauty of a most natural kind.*

An old door, gate, or small building, so often an eyesore, acquires the distinction of an antique when decorated with a climber. Clematis montana, *a plant of exuberant freshness, lends an air of patience and purpose to what might otherwise be discarded as ugly. In growing away into surrounding plants it creates a coherence which will be as effective when the flowers have gone and only the foliage remains.*

such as *Skimmia*. I prefer the pure species, with its sky-blue, hanging flowers, but the variety 'Frances Rivis', which has larger flowers of a deeper blue, is the more common form and it is a fine vigorous plant. *C. macropetala* is the Asian equivalent of *C. alpina*. It is similar in growth and flower, liking to adorn a fence or low wall, such as you might have at the boundary of a patio. It follows *C. alpina* in flower and crosses from spring into summer. A pink form, 'Markhams Pink', is a good plant that finds favor with some, but the blue of the species is unbeatable. *C. armandii* flowers just about between the two previous ones. It is evergreen and just a little tender and it should not be pruned at all. It has flowers of almost 8cm/3in across, which are creamy-white and scented.

C. *montana* is extemely vigorous, and so if wall space is at a premium, consider growing it into a tree, and you will be rewarded year after year by great clouds of neat flowers in white or shades of pink. Among its many forms is 'Alexander', which is white and scented, and *rubens* which has pink flowers and bronze shoots.

Harbingers of summer

As spring turns to summer, the Californian Lilacs begin their great show of blue. These plants are, in fact, not lilacs at all, but belong to the genus *Ceanothus*. They are not all hardy, but a great many can be grown in cool-temperate climates where the winters are on the easy side. Above all else, what they must have is sun and good drainage; apart from that, they are not particular as to soil, although they are not partial to hot, thin soils closely laid over limestone.

Ceanothus can be had in flower for six months of the year, while one or two have a tendency to carry on flowering right through mild winters. One that does this is the spring-flowering *C. arboreus*, usually grown as the variety 'Trewithen Blue'. It is a tall shrub of about 4.5m/15ft and it has lilaclike clusters of dark blue flowers during midspring.

Among the small-leafed species is *C. impressus* and it is one of the very best. Its habit is extremely dense and its tiny leaves are indented where the veins occur. The color of the abundantly borne flowers is one of the deepest and richest blue and it is fairly hardy. Flowering in the second half of spring, when blue flowers are not really expected, it is a true gem whose appearance as a neat, evergreen shrub is also attractive throughout the year. Another with a very different character is *C. papillosus*, a tiny shrub with flowers again of deep blue and slightly larger leaves with sticky, glandular papillae on their upper surfaces. The effect is not matt, but furrily glossy.

C. 'Cascade' is a more open, twiggy, evergreen plant, which, for sheer mass of flower, has few equals in the garden. *C. gloriosus* is almost completely prostrate, a habit shared with *C. prostratus*, and *C. rigidus* is so compact that its shape tends to be globelike. With such a variety of form, and with one or two having white flowers, the genus is of utmost value in taking the garden through that transitional period of late spring into summer.

Ceanothus is a genus of such variety of form and spread of flowering season that it is of the utmost value in taking the garden through from late spring into summer. The spring-flowering C. arboreus is wonderfully free-blooming and its evergreen leaves are an adornment throughout the year. The variety 'Mist' is of a light, vivid blue that reflects the spring sky.

SUMMER

*In high summer, stillness reigns, with the waxing and waning
of flowers against a constancy of rich, mature foliage.*

SUMMER IS A SEASON OF profound but subtle change. Early on there is still much of the freshness and soft colors of spring. As time passes, gardens become charged with brighter, stronger colors and with hints of the exotic, while foliage takes on deeper, more somber hues.

The light is different, too. Whereas in spring it is clear, fresh and vibrant, in summer it becomes heavier and somehow more dense, even though it may be unbearably bright. Distances look greater and shades of green become darker and rather less distinct. And then comes the germ of decline in late summer and the brooding hint of autumn colors in the foliage.

It is part of the gardener's art to minimize these changes without diminishing the beauty of summer. You should try to retain some of the exuberance of spring while deflecting the lurking sense of things coming to an end. There is, of course, an enormous choice of plants that look spectacular in summer, but it is very important to be selective. You should be careful not to swamp the garden with summer-flowering plants at the expense of other seasons.

Seasonal continuity

Primulas afford us yet another opportunity to breach the barriers between seasons. Although they are generally thought of in terms of spring, there are groups of primulas that flower in succession from early summer until late. They have all those qualities we expect from spring plants and serve wonderfully to postpone the realization that the year is on its way downhill.

The Candelabra Primulas are so-called because their stems, which vary from 30cm/12in high in some species to 75cm/30in in others, carry their flowers in concentric whorls, one on top of the other, with large spaces between them. They appreciate moisture and some shade, although they enjoy full sun in really wet situations; they thrive in good, ordinary soils that do not dry out, such as are found around shrubs.

Indeed, if you grow a succession of primulas in this way, a group of spring-flowering shrubs will be a colorful place for several weeks after their flowering is over.

There are about ten species that are easily grown in most gardens and some are listed on p. 157. Their colors range from deep purple, as in *Primula anisodora*, through reds – *P. pulverulenta* for example, which also has a shell-pink variety called 'Bartley Strain' – to yellow and deep orange. It is worthwhile trying to avoid growing the reds where there is a chance of any rhododendrons with red flowers still blooming, as there will be a nasty clash (one of the few cases of "natural" flowers clashing); the gold and orange ones will not offend in this respect. Candelabra Primulas are very easy to grow from seed provided that, as with all primulas, the seed is not covered when it is sown.

The Sikkimensis Group of primulas resemble large cowslips and are unabashed moisture-lovers. They are pearls beyond price for the edges of the water garden or for any spot that is shady and really damp. *P. sikkimensis* itself is an elegant plant, with a stem about 46cm/18in high, from which dangle light cream-yellow flowers with a gentle scent. Its large cousin *P. florindae* is

RIGHT *Even after the lushness of summer has gone, the combination of a rich planting design, the use of evergreens, contrasting shapes, changing levels and a beautiful water feature ensures that the secret, almost magical atmosphere of this garden will remain throughout the year. One straight line at the edge of the pond links the garden to the line of the house – itself a vital part of the ascending levels that characterize the garden and give it its air of seclusion. The house is dramatically bare of plants in contrast to the walls below, which are thickly clothed and are a backdrop for the diagonal march of clipped evergreens. This is all reflected in the water, whose edges are for the most part overlapped by conifers, grasses and other plants that will play their part all the year round.*

LEFT *The Candelabra Primula* P. japonica *does well in damp spots. Its color is strong, but is perfectly accompanied by the soft green of ferns, including the Shuttlecock Fern,* Matteuccia struthiopteris.

very similar except for its being about twice as large in all its parts; not for nothing is it called the Giant Himalayan Cowslip. *P. florindae* starts flowering when *P. sikkimensis* leaves off, and the two provide almost three months of flower as there are early and late-flowering forms of each.

Very different from these is *P. capitata*. This fairly small plant has wrinkled, farinose leaves and tight, ball-like heads of flowers which are blue-purple, and each has a yellow eye. It likes a leafy soil with a little shade and is ideal for the outskirts of groups of shrubs. It should be planted in drifts so that it shows up, because it will flower until the end of summer (there is a deep purple form which extends into early autumn and one called 'Early Lilac' which starts at the end of spring) and it is worth accentuating.

Springlike foliage

Plants that keep the crisp lightness of spring in their foliage are all-important. The Hart's-Tongue Fern, for instance, not only retains its salady glossiness right through the summer, but also by its very nature is redolent of the cool, moist floor of the forest where spring things happen. It is a plant for placing in drifts among trees and will no doubt have as its companions the crinkled, still young leaves of the primulas.

Small trees can also provide springlike foliage that will continue well into the latter part of summer. *Robinia pseudoacacia* 'Frisia' is a tree that will fit into small gardens as well as large ones, and in a garden of any size at all its use should be sparing and directed toward per-petuating freshness. Its richly golden foliage does not fade from bud-burst to leaf-fall, and its place should be among or in front of darker leaves. If you want to repeat the statement somewhere else and your garden is not a big one, do it with something else, not with another *Robinia*. The softer tones of *Gleditsia triacanthos* 'Sunburst', with a hint of apple-green in the gold, will do the same job but will appear more like an echo of the bright color of the *Robinia*.

ABOVE Robinia pseudo-acacia 'Frisia' is used to perfection here, with the bright, sunlit gold of its leaves against the dark walls and tiles.

LEFT While summer flowers come and go, bright foliage is of longer-lasting importance. Here an old rose scrambles among leafy shrubs including the light-green- and purple-leaved forms of Acer palmatum. The conifer will retain its color during autumn and into winter.

Summer-flowering trees

As well as trees with light foliage softening the summer garden, there are also those that flower at this time of year, brightening the often rather somber greens of the surrounding trees. Some are very good all-seasons plants and there are examples for all sizes of garden.

Small gardens
Best for bridging the seasons from spring to summer is Styrax japonica. Its branches, covered with tidily arranged foliage, are horizontal and each one has, along the entire length of its lower

surface, dozens of white, snowdroplike flowers hanging down so that a tiered effect like a chandelier is produced. Its trunk is straight and slender, and the disposition of its branches make it attractive at all times. As a lawn specimen it is perfect and needs no companions to increase its appeal.

Embothrium coccineum var. lanceolatum 'Norquinco Valley' is a tree which often breaks into branches very low down and it does not make a good single specimen. The chief reason for recommending it for the all-seasons garden is that if you have a lime-free soil and a reasonably mild climate, it is so beautiful when in flower that it is impossible to resist, having groups of tubular, vividly scarlet flowers all along each branch. Its slightly twiggy appearance can be disguised by growing it with a green background; mature camellias would be ideal, or eucryphias. In such a situation the flame color of the "Chilean Fire Bush" shows up to its very best advantage. Two or three planted in a tight group in front of dark green foliage will produce a spectacular and unforgettable effect. The plant is evergreen, so does not spoil the picture with bare branches in winter.

Koelreuteria paniculata, the Golden Rain Tree, is another good summer-flowering tree. This sun-loving, medium-sized tree, which tends to be broader than high at maturity, grows to a height of 15m/50ft. It has purple-brown bark with narrow, orange fissures. The true glory of the species is the enormous, pyramidal panicles of golden flowers that develop during early summer, but its foliage is also striking. The leaves are boldly pinnate, each leaflet being about 10cm/4in long and the whole leaf can be more than 45cm/18in in a well-grown specimen. In a warm enough climate (or a good summer in a cooler one) the flowers are followed by large, bladderlike fruits, while the soft gold autumn color is best where there is a sharp drop in temperature later in the year. As a centerpiece of a small, rather formal layout it will introduce a wonderfully exotic note.

63

Larger gardens

Boldness of foliage, extraordinary seed pods, and a touch of the exotic are also characteristic of the catalpas, but these are for the slightly larger garden. They flower later in the summer and do well in any soil. *Catalpa bignonioides*, the Indian Bean Tree, has large, bold, heart-shaped leaves and white, foxglovelike flowers with purple markings. The long, beanlike seed pods give it its vernacular name and extend its interest into the autumn. Its habit of growth is wide-spreading but *C.b.* 'Aurea' is neater and is a very effective foliage tree. The leaves are even larger, with a velvety sheen, and are the color of old gold. A dark background suits this plant very well and it is a first-class subject for use in a gold color theme.

Magnolia sinensis flowers in early summer and, although it is rather a wide-spreading small tree, its white, saucer-shaped flowers are beautiful and have a strong almost lemony scent. It is not a plant for small gardens but it has the great virtue among magnolias of being able to be grown even on the most limey of soils. While its flowers are pendent, those of M. *sieboldii* are set sideways so that, to quote Millais, they 'look you in the face'. Its habit is somewhat similar to M. *sinensis*, but unlike that tree it is a lime-hater.

Perhaps the best summer-flowering magnolia is M. *grandiflora*. Its flowers are enormous and are very effective even though they occur intermittently over a period of two months or so. They are creamy white, almost light yellow, and have a spicy scent. M. *grandiflora* has magnificent foliage which makes it one of the most desirable of garden plants; the leaves are up to 25cm/10in long, very leathery, and are a dark, glossy green on their upper surfaces. They are covered on the undersides with deep red-brown felt which disappears as the leaf ages, although it is absent or nearly so in some varieties.

It is a tall tree in nature, but is usually more compact in cultivation, especially where snow occurs, as the weight of snow on its branches tends to break them. If this happens they grow

Magnolia grandiflora

Magnolia sieboldii

away again very rapidly from vigorous new shoots but a true tree-shape is seldom attained. For this reason it is often grown trained against a wall and indeed the foliage is set off better by a wall than by any other background.

Shrubs

It is in summer that you will have the most difficulty in finding good flowering shrubs because, although there are plenty of shrubs that flower in summer, there are not all that many with all-seasons appeal. It seems a pity to dismiss favorites like *Philadelphus* and *Deutzia* out of hand, but they really are lacking in out-of-flower qualities. They are by no means alone in this, and careful choice of summer subjects must be paramount.

Rhododendrons for small gardens

If you are the owner of a small garden who feels that even a very few rhododendrons are likely to be too much for your space, you need not turn your head away from summer-flowering ones. Some of them are small plants, which have great

Magnolias
Magnolia grandiflora 'Exmouth' *is a beautiful evergreen of large shrub stature, whose enormous, scented, cream flowers are mostly borne in late summer. Its foliage is always beautiful and resists a great deal of frost.* Magnolia sieboldii *is a small tree, or more often a large shrub. Its flowers are pure white, cup-shaped, long-stalked, and have a delicious scent, and its stamens form a crimson disk at the center of the flower. The plant flowers a few at a time from late spring to late summer and is very frost-hardy.*

Few shrubs can match the beauty of the Smoke Bush, Cotinus coggygria, in late summer. Its inflorescences are pink throughout, including the stalks, and they are produced with an abundance that makes the plant appear as if shrouded in a filmy gauze of pink. Later, the pink turns to gray, so that the shrub seems clouded in smoke; later still, the leaves turn bright yellow, red or sometimes both together. Few plants provide such billowing wealth for so long a time.

impact for their size, and will fit into small gardens. *Rhododendron nakaharai* is a prostrate, evergreen azalea which makes little carpets of dense foliage with almost stemless flowers in pink, red, or orange-red in mid- to late summer. It should be grown in a very peaty soil in a raised bed to be seen at its best, although it can be massed in front of other small shrubs. The best form is one called 'Mariko'. *R. occidentale* is a deciduous azalea, whose hybrids flower late in the spring, but the species itself is midsummer flowering and the forms now in cultivation are first-class. The dominant note in the flower color is cream-white with yellow markings and there are some suggestions of pink. 'Leonard Frisbie' is reliable if rather slow-growing.

Later still is another deciduous azalea, *R. prunifolium*. It is hardy to −10°F/−23°C but it needs plenty of warmth to make it thrive. It flowers in late summer and the search for a site in full sun, but where the soil will not become too dry, is worth all the trouble. The color is normally a flaming orange-red, although there are dark red forms.

These small deciduous azaleas have strong colors in the main and might at first sight seem difficult to place. In the larger garden they can be planted to great effect in good soil on the sunny sides of fairly large trees, perhaps with under-plantings of polyanthus to provide spring color. Their own foliage tints will add to the autumn scene later on. In small gardens they look well when associated with spring-flowering dwarf rhododendrons, where they will provide bright color long after their evergreen neighbors have finished flowering.

Summer whites

White is a dominant color among summer-flowering shrubs. *Eucryphia* is a genus consisting of plants with white flowers only, and *E. lucida* is the most dainty and about the earliest flower-ing. It has small, simple, oblong leaves which congregate to make the plant a thing of exquisite beauty throughout the year. Its flowers are about 5cm/2in across, and sweetly scented. It has in common with the others of the genus a liking for having its roots shaded from sun and if it is grown with low-growing plants at its feet it will tend to remain furnished with foliage and flowers right down to their level. Where heaths merge into the rest of the garden is a good place, especially as they, too, require lime-free soils.

Eucryphia × nymansensis 'Nymansay' is larger, later-flowering and hardier than *E. lucida*. The gray-green leaves are either simple or compound on the same plant and are much larger. Out of

RIGHT *A pretty summer house surrounded by cool green foliage makes a feature of a shady corner. Apart from a splash of bright color in summer, the effect will change little in other seasons.*

Viburnums
LEFT *Most viburnums have white flowers, and those of* V. plicatum *var.* tomento-sum *'Mariesii' belong to a shrub with striking foliage and shape.*

BELOW *The large flowers of* Eucryphia × nymansensis *'Nymansay' last for almost a month and can so cover the plant that, at a distance, the foliage disappears.*

flower its best use is as a background for plants such as embothriums, but when in bloom it is one of the glories of late summer and early autumn. It is a large shrub and when it wreathes all its branches with 6cm/2½in flowers it turns itself into a column of shining white. Trees should be in the background, otherwise the effect is dissipated.

Viburnum is a large genus which has pink members but is predominantly white. The summer-flowering species include some which are among the top class of garden plants – they are hardy, beautiful in flower, and display good form and character.

By very early in the summer the forms of *V. plicatum* are in play. The truly wild form, *V.p.* var. *tomentosum*, is in some ways the best of them. It is a wide-spreading shrub whose branches are horizontal and which carry, in double rows all along their lengths, heads of white flowers that have a resemblance, on a small scale, to those of lacecap hydrangeas. The effect is like a layered wedding-cake and it is an inveterate show-stopper. What is more, its bright green leaves are pleated (hence *plicatum*) and very different from anything else. Out of leaf, the branch structure is distinguished and looks, once again, wedding-cakelike when adorned with hoar-frost. The cultivar 'Mariesii' is even more pronounced in the horizontal arrangement of branches and is the form most often met with. The striking way in which the branches of these viburnums are held makes them plants that should not be hidden in winter but used to enhance the form of other plants. A nearby weeping pear, for example, will appear all the more pendulous next to the horizontal array of the viburnum, while a couple of conical conifers in the neighborhood will benefit similarly.

Viburnum odoratissimum is one of the most valuable of summer-flowering shrubs for all-year-round excellence. It is evergreen and flowers at the end of summer, but is slightly tender and needs wall protection in other than mild areas. In flower it has large panicles of white, scented blooms which are conically arranged. This is a magnificent shrub with large, glossy, leathery leaves which can be up to 20cm/8in long. These striking leaves are held on petioles that are thick and tan-colored and which hold the leaves out at a bold angle.

A marvelous shrub that flowers from spring into summer is *Cornus kousa* var. *chinensis*. Like the spring-flowering American Dogwoods, it has the same 'flowers', consisting of white bracts, and these are displayed along the tops of branches which are nearly horizontal. Its effect is somewhat similar to *Viburnum plicatum* and their flowering times can coincide so that, planted a little distance from each other, they can complement one another and create a most pleasing comparison.

A summer comparison
An all-seasons garden in which shapes of plants, contours and features are more important than flower color. Here the graceful curves of the path and the edges of the water contrast with the straight lines of the house and the rugged shapes of the carefully placed stones. The harmonious framework of the garden will remain unchanged throughout the year. In summer the effect is green and tranquil, while a dramatic fiery note is introduced by autumn color.

White and blue

Ceanothus is another genus whose species bridge the seasons. C. 'Gloire de Versailles' has large panicles of light blue during summer and autumn. It makes a very good wall shrub, especially when associated with a white clematis such as 'Henryi', whose flowers will coincide with the blue of the ceanothus.

White and blue is a combination that I find hard to resist and I am in great danger of over-doing the association between *Convolvulus cneorum* and two of the evergreen ceanothus. In a large garden, the spreading mounds of *Ceanothus thyrsiflorus* var. *repens* will flower at the same time as the convolvulus enjoys its main flush of large, white bells.

For smaller gardens, the arrangement can consist of just two or three of each genus, but here the much smaller *Ceanothus* 'Blue Mound' is appropriate. Not only are the flowers comple-mentary; all the year round you will have the most stunning contrast between the tightly packed, deep green foliage of the ceanothus and the shining silver of the convolvulus.

Massed color

In summer, it is very difficult indeed to produce the massed color effects from shrubs that are possible during the spring. This is in part because of the natures of the summer-flowering shrubs, which do not lend themselves to mass planting as, for example, the spring azaleas do.

Ceanothus veitchianus is possibly the hardiest ceanothus and cannot be matched for wealth of flower and for the richness of its blue in early summer. A true all-seasons shrub, its evergreen leaves are dark and glossy.

Cistuses are one of the few exceptions to this and they can be planted in drifts or closely set groups with great effect.

The cistuses are very summery shrubs which, when grown in cooler countries, recall times spent under a hotter sun and bluer skies. They are mostly rounded bushes of 1m/3ft or so in height with a few that are a lot smaller. Their flowers are produced in such quantities that, although each one only lasts for a day, they are covered in blooms for up to two months. They are evergreen plants and among them is a great diversity of foliage. Almost all of them make pleasant features in the garden when out of flower and they are very useful because they will grow well on dry banks on just about any soil, no matter how thin, and never suffer from drought.

If you want to use just one cistus and to plant several in a group, one that will look well is *Cistus laurifolius*, which has the advantage of being the hardiest. Its flowers are white, 7.6cm/ 3in across, and keep on coming into late summer. On sunny days it is one of the plants that contribute to the aromatic atmosphere of the garden; its leaves send an incenselike perfume into the air over a considerable distance. One of its hybrids is C. × *cyprius* whose flowers are even larger and are borne in clusters of up to six. It is not as hardy as its parent; however, it will still stand severe winters. Its other parent is C. *ladanifer*, whose singly held flowers are larger again – up to 10cm/4in wide – and have large maroon blotches at the bases of the petals. All these white-flowered cistuses are among the most beautiful of garden plants. Their large, crumpled-tissue-paper flowers are perfectly matched for style, shape and carriage by those of the Modern Shrub Rose 'Frühlingsgold', which is of a soft yellow, or by the silvery lilac of the Rugosa Rose 'Conrad F. Meyer'. The roses will also add an element of height to a planting of cistuses.

Although I have dismissed *Philadelphus* in general, I must make one exception and recommend *P. coronarius* 'Aureus' as a companion for

ABOVE Convolvulus cneorum *is of most value in the all-seasons garden for its evergreen, silver leaves. Although flowering in early summer, it can produce flowers intermittently for months when well suited. It is my favorite plant.*

LEFT Cistus ladanifer, *the "Gum Cistus" – one of a genus of plants which, although rather tender, can be relied upon to flower all summer and to look attractive all year round where severe winters are not too prolonged.*

Most members of Philadelphus are not good all-seasons plants, having little to recommend them when out of flower. A notable exception is P. coronarius 'Aureus' whose leaves are a bright gold, becoming a little more green in late summer.

the cistuses. It is a shrub of medium size which is clothed to the ground with bright golden foliage and which is wonderful when seen at a distance among the darker shades of green. Close to, the gray-green of the cistuses surrounding it make a further contrast, and their long flowering season makes up for the shortness of the lives of the white, scented flowers of the philadelphus.

Heaths and heathers

While most of the summer plants that we have considered so far bring spring into summer, the heaths and heathers start in early summer and continue right through the autumn and into winter. Even during the two months of the year when there are few of them in flower, their foliage of green, gold, gray and russet maintains a cheery and beautiful picture for the whole of the twelve months. However, this will only happen if the plants are occasionally cut back in spring before growth starts. Doing this encourages new growth from lower down and stops the plants from becoming woody and straggly.

Heaths and heathers associate well, as mentioned, with dwarf and slow-growing conifers, which introduce shapes other than the humps of the heaths and heathers. Because they are moorland plants, it is appropriate to plant some of the dwarf or prostrate willows, such as *Salix apoda*, *S. hastata* 'Wehrhahnii' and *S. retusa*, at the edges of beds, where their ground-hugging or gnarled structure can be easily seen and the contrast made all the more striking.

Erica cinerea is very hardy. There are about thirty good varieties and their colors range from the almost black purple of 'Velvet Night' through lilacs, reds and pinks to the white of 'Alba Minor' and 'Alba Major'. Their flowering season is a little shorter than the other heaths and they only just see the beginning of autumn.

The Dorset Heath, *Erica ciliaris*, carries its fairly large flowers at the ends of branches which are thickly furnished with hairy leaves and are very attractive in themselves. There are only a handful of varieties, mostly red or pink, while 'Stoborough' is white.

Erica tetralix is notable for its gray, often silvery foliage and its dense heads of flowers which range from red to white. The last of the summer heaths is the Cornish Heath, *E. vagans*, which has the biggest flower-heads of all – long, slightly drooping racemes of white, rose and cerise according to variety. It and the preceding species flower well into the autumn.

Summer-flowering heaths are best grown in a natural arrangement, and in this garden they have been thoughtfully planted where a sunny slope meets a belt of trees. The different kinds of foliage and varying shapes of the heaths ensure that this will never be a dull part of the garden, especially if planted for successional flowering. Conifers are ideal companions for heaths but, as here, they should be used with care and not planted with the regularity of chessmen. The grassy path, winding its way past the heaths and away into the trees, is just right for such a setting and it provides a feeling of continuity.

Climbers

The genus *Clematis* is perfect for the all-seasons garden. You cannot have too many of these versatile plants, and in summer – as in every season – their use for gardening in depth and, especially, for extending the flowering seasons of spring-flowering shrubs is unequaled.

There are so many large-flowered varieties of clematis that choice is a matter of taste and color preference – chiefly the latter, as, although the flowers are large and are developed a long way from their wild ancestors, they are always of a form that fits in anywhere. They are happy to be grown, and look well, with other climbers, too, particularly roses.

Among the species and species hybrid roses are some of the best of summer-flowering climbing plants. Many of them are very large, but there are some that can be accommodated into comparatively small gardens. To a large extent it is a matter of how they are grown. The spectacular, blood-red, single-flowered *Rosa moyesii* can be trained over a pergola or an arch and stopped when the long shoots have reached the required length. It is a plant with great all-seasons appeal, having enormous, bright red, flask-shaped fruits, and it associates beautifully with white or pale blue clematis. (In larger gardens you can grow it as a shrub with its shoots arched over, and pegged to the ground so as to produce flowers all along their lengths.)

Rosa dupontii is similarly versatile and its marvelously fragrant, large flowers, pink at first and then turning white, can be succeeded by the small, blue ones of *Clematis campaniflora* before the fruits of the roses become prominent.

Many old-fashioned roses have climbing forms and it is on a wall or over an arch that they are seen at their best. The climbing form of 'Souvenir de la Malmaison' is almost unbeatable. Its large, flesh-pink, fully quartered blooms with their wonderful scent keep coming until early autumn and to stand surrounded by them is a lovely experience. 'Gruss an Teplitz' is deep crimson and loosely double and it, too, has a fabulous scent and a long flowering period, and it can be induced to climb with no difficulty. The two together on an arch, each growing from the opposite side but mingling their blooms at the top, make an unforgettable picture.

A clematis will often flower abundantly if given the right growing conditions. Here, the flowering stems are in sun, while the roots are shaded by the little chrysanthemum and Alchemilla mollis.

RIGHT Rosa moyesii *is an excellent summer-flowering climber. It grows vigorously, flowers just once with great intensity, but then bears large, scarlet flask-shaped fruits for weeks on end.*

BELOW Solanum crispum *'Glasnevin' is also a strong grower, but needs a sheltered sunny wall. In mild areas it can be used to climb over buildings or fences. It is long-flowering – from midsummer to early autumn.*

Support for climbers

While walls, trees, pergolas and arches are all good sites for gardening in depth, all-seasons gardeners should also regard anything that is above soil level as a vehicle for a climber. You can transform old tree stumps that are too large to be removed without great expense into positive garden features by planting climbing or scrambling things over them. Even some of the most exotic treasures can lend themselves to such a mundane task. *Asteranthera ovata* is a beautiful Chilean creeper with red, two-lipped flowers. In mild gardens it will clothe a wall or the trunk of a tree, rather after the manner of ivy, but its love of shade makes it specially suitable for hiding tree stumps, as they are usually to be found in shady positions.

Sheds and outhouses can acquire an air of rusticity if they are submerged under the tangle of a well-developed jasmine. *Jasminum × stephanense* has pink, scented flowers for most of the summer, and you can grow it intermingled with the stems of *J. officinale*, the common white jasmine, whose flowers last even longer and whose scent is really powerful.

Shady walls can easily be clothed with ivies or the ubiquitous *Clematis* 'Nellie Moser', but to find high-class flowering plants that will be happy there can be difficult. Two that are ideal are *Lapageria rosea* and *Berberidopsis corallina*; however they do not look well together. *Lapageria* is one of the most beautiful of all climbers with large, well-shaped flowers of a waxy, rose-crimson color and whose leaves are evergreen, gray-green and leathery with a pleasing, round heart shape. The leaves of *Berberidopsis*, too, are leathery and heart-shaped, but dark green and there the resemblance ends, as the flowers are smaller and shaped like little, bright red balls and hang in many-flowered clusters on long stalks. Grow the two by all means, but do not put them together, otherwise they will create one of those rare but spectacular clashes that can totally ruin the qualities and great attractions of such fine plants.

Roses

The shrub roses play an important part in filling what is sometimes called the 'summer gap' – a gap in flower-bearing that occurs in gardens where the emphasis is on woody plants – and none are more beautiful than the so-called old-fashioned roses.

There are several groups of old roses, but in the all-seasons garden, and especially for small gardens, where the maximum benefit has to be obtained from every plant, the remontant, or repeat-flowering, roses are best. What they all have in common is character as plants; they do not have to be pruned hard each year – so they do not look ugly when out of flower, as the Hybrid Teas do – and they can develop as shrubs in their own right. (The same is true of many of the Modern Shrub Roses.)

The flowers range from singles, which have an elegance all of their own, through semidoubles to full doubles of a kind called 'Quartered'; here the flowers are cup-shaped and so filled with petals that they are packed into whorls, often four in number.

The Bourbon and Hybrid Perpetual Roses have the longest seasons, starting in midsummer and continuing into the autumn. The range of colors is limited compared with modern roses, but then some of the more garish modern tones are difficult to fit in with other shrubs. The soft, deep reds, the white and the creamy hues are truly wonderful, and varying degrees of striping and streaking help to create a wide variation on a restricted palette. The old-fashioned roses are also without exception the possessors of powerful fragrances. To walk among them is to experience all the subtleties of the perfumier's art, as no two roses have exactly the same scent.

When the roses begin to flower, their role is dominant and any underplanting becomes merely a distraction. However, low-growing plants that flower before the roses are highly desirable in the all-seasons context. The white hardy geranium, G. sylvaticum var. album, is ideal, as any of its flowers that come later cannot cause a clash. Dicentras on the other hand have a range of colors in reds and pinks that actually complement the rose colors and they will flower both before and during the blooming of the roses.

The use of roses among other shrubs overcomes the predominance of white among summer-flowering plants. Not only that; the white flowers will not detract from those of the roses but will emphasize their color tones. Thr occasional eucryphia and white spiraea gain from association with old roses and the roses derive benefit from them in turn.

Not that yellow should be left out. It is a color that is absent among the old roses but you can find it in the Modern Shrub Roses. It can also be supplied by planting Hypericum 'Hidcote' or the better but slightly tender 'Rowallane'. These shrubs will attain the same dimensions as most of the roses and can be planted in close association with them.

Summer is unthinkable without roses, but perhaps the all-seasons approach will help to see them used as integral elements of the garden rather than as isolated regiments of cosseted, overbred invalids.

Rosa rugosa 'Alba' (below left) has one main flowering, but its fruits and foliage make it a valuable all-seasons shrub. The Modern Shrub Rose 'Golden Wings' (below) is perpetual-flowering and is regarded as one of the best roses ever raised. The Hybrid Musk 'Ballerina' (bottom) flowers all summer and into the autumn and makes a wonderful low hedge.

Rosa helenae (left) is a Chinese species with large white, scented flowers which are followed by longlasting pear-shaped fruits that are fairly large and of an orange-red color. It needs space in a larger garden to display its full beauty.

Rosa filipes 'Kiftsgate' (above) is a beautiful rose, but rather too rampant for all but the largest gardens, where it will romp among the tree tops, making great waterfalls of white flowers in mid-summer. Its myriad, small fruits are light yellow-orange.

Herbaceous plants

The all-seasons garden should, of course, consist almost exclusively of perennial plants. Most of them will be woody, and will give a permanent structure to the garden, but herbaceous perennials are also very useful for adding new color. However, there is no reason whatever why annuals should be excluded completely. Many of them are very lovely, but their beauty is short-lived, and a garden that makes much use of annuals will be very bare for a great deal of the year, and it will also have to be 're-made' anew every year.

Perennials
Herbaceous perennials are important in the all-seasons garden. As they expand their stems and leaves, they will hide other things that have either made their contribution for the year or are to be kept deliberately as surprises for other times. You might, for instance, grow *Hemerocallis*, the 'Day-Lilies', among Candelabra Primulas. They are not lilies but are so called because their flowers are trumpet-shaped and their colors, variations of red, yellow and pink, are lilylike. You will not want to cut down the tall stems of the primulas after they have flowered because it will be a lot of work and, besides, you want the seed, so you should allow the even taller stems of the day-lilies to grow up among them and effectively hide them, or certainly camouflage their presence. What is more, you will have extended the flowering span of that piece of ground by as much as three months, bringing it to a total of six if short-stemmed daffodils come before the primulas – and even more if there are a few snowdrops before the daffodils.

LEFT *'Pink Damask' is one of a very large range of* Hemerocallis. *The 'Day Lilies' provide a major source of summer color and can be grown anywhere in the garden.*

RIGHT *A beautiful pot planted with* Nicotiana *'Lime Green Strain' will decorate a patio in summer and will make the evening air softly scented.*

Annuals

A great deal of the pleasure of summer gardening is obtained from annuals and they have a role to play in providing color and scent, not only as fillers among shrubs which have not attained much size, but also as plants in their own right.

Near the house it is very pleasant indeed to have patches of Night-scented Stock and nicotianas, whose perfumes help to make an evening's sitting on the patio such a lovely experience, and hanging baskets, planted with annuals and the occasional plant of *Jasminum polyanthum* look just right when placed by the house. There is little wrong with, for example, having a few sweet peas growing on the fence to provide cut flowers for the dinner-table, so long as you remember always that a garden filled with annuals can never be an all-seasons garden – it is all a matter of balance and proportion.

Summer bulbs

The role of bulbs in summer is rather different from that which they play in spring. Whereas earlier they are a major factor in the color design and are best planted in large groups or drifts, bulbs in summer are an accessory to the general colorfulness and a means of continuing the contribution made by other plants in spring. By being planted between or among spring-flowering shrubs, they take over from the flowers of the shrubs themselves.

Lilies are perfect for growing among those shrubs that have finished flowering by the early weeks of the season. The reason for this is that the great majority of them like to be planted in cool, moist soil which is rich in vegetable matter but so that they can grow up into the sun. They must not, however, become crowded-out by

BELOW *The great, trumpet-shaped flowers of* Lilium regale *lend summer color and powerful scent to plantings of spring-flowering shrubs. The bulbs can be planted directly into the ground or started in pots and then planted while in growth.*

other plants and it is a matter of striking a balance so that they receive support – and shelter from the hot sun – for their stems, but do not become starved or overgrown. Grown in isolation they are easily blown over and will die out after a few years. An exception to this is *Lilium candidum*, the Madonna Lily, which will succeed in the open border and which will grow well in limestone. It must still be sheltered from wind, though.

Of all the bulbs that you can call on to assist you in your quest for year-round color, lilies will do the most efficient and thoroughly satisfactory job, completely transforming shrubs like azaleas and smaller rhododendrons whose main contributions have already been made. Lilies have a stateliness that few plants can match, and those that are scented are so much the better.

Among these are *L. regale*, whose very large, trumpet-shaped flowers – sometimes twenty or more on a stem – are white with a yellow throat and deep pink markings on the outside bases of the petals. 'Royal Gold' is just that, and the two forms look very well in groups of the two colors. The stems are often up to 1.5m/5ft tall and this brings the blooms up to a level where their exquisite perfume can best be appreciated. *L. regale* is so easily grown that it should be in everyone's garden, including those on limestone; but do not give it much shade. *L. auratum* is called the Golden-rayed Lily because its enormous, funnel-shaped flowers have varying amounts of markings in yellow, or sometimes, red. It flowers right at the end of summer and it is vital that the flower heads should be able to reach the full sunlight.

If you have groups of low-growing shrubs facing south, then the lilies among them will receive the maximum possible sunlight while still having their roots shaded. This combination

Summer flowers
The Turkscap Lily, Lilium martagon has the virtue of being extremely hardy and easy to grow and naturalize. Crinum × powellii does best by a sunny wall, where it can be left alone to increase into a sizable colony. Agapanthus will grow and flower well in sun or shade.

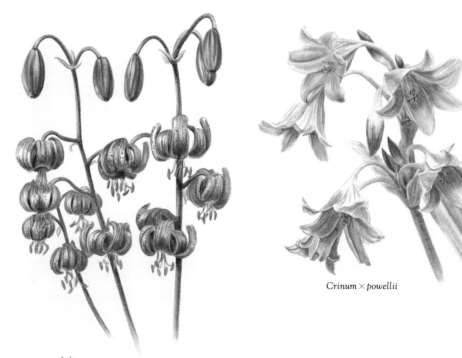

Lilium martagon

Crinum × powellii

Agapanthus

is especially important in the stem-rooting group of lilies of which *L. auratum* is a member because the roots which grow from the bottoms of the stems would not survive heat and dryness. It is, in any case, always a good idea to cover them with earth as they form.

The Turkscap Lilies are very different in appearance from the Trumpet Lilies. In these the petals are reflexed and rolled backward so as to give the appearance of a certain type of turban. *L. martagon* is the commonest and it is easy enough to grow. Better by far, though, is *L. hansonii*. Both are unbothered by alkaline soil and both are good garden plants but *L. hansonii* is larger in flower, taller and has a lovely orange-yellow color.

Crinum × powellii is a plant whose flowers are not unlike those of a lily but which otherwise does not resemble one at all. Its bulb is enormous with a very long neck which gives rise to long, strap-shaped foliage and stout, tough stems on which are large, trumpet-shaped blooms – usually pink or, more rarely, white. Each stem has many flowers and what makes the flowering season of the plant such a long one is that they open in succession. It associates beautifully with *Agapanthus*, a plant that looks as though it ought to grow from a bulb and does not. This late-summer-flowering plant has open, wide heads of hanging flowers which are vividly blue (except in the white forms).

Other summer bulbs tend not to be suitable for the all-seasons garden. They are mostly tender and need lifting and replanting or to need warm conditions with mild winters.

Heralds of autumn

Hydrangeas must be included when summer-flowering plants are discussed, but they are truly autumnal in nature and can be said to bridge over the two seasons more effectively than any other group of plants.

Their flowering season proper starts after midsummer, builds up to a climax as summer turns to autumn, and then continues into early winter when the substance of the flowers changes from silkiness to waxiness, and the colors alter. The blues become *eau-de-nil*, the reds turn to a brown-maroon, and the whites take on green tones. Hydrangeas are woodland plants. Some of them are really large – up to 2.5m/8ft high and 1.8m/6ft wide – and the fact that they hardly ever look right when planted singly means that only a few of them are good subjects for the small garden.

In general, the mopheads – those with large, ball-like heads of flowers – are smaller than the lacecaps, whose flowers are arranged in flat heads with large, sterile florets surrounding the central clusters of tiny, fertile ones. A group of 'Vibraye', an early-flowering, sky-blue mop-head, can be planted in a fairly small garden against, for example, the foliage of earlier-flowering shrubs.

Hydrangea quercifolia *is so called because its leaves closely resemble those of some American Oaks. Its late summer flowers are very pretty, but the magnificent autumn colors of its foliage make it an asset for much longer. Semishade suits it well and it dislikes dry conditions.*

The climbing hydrangea, H. petiolaris, *can attain a height of 20m/60ft on a suitable host tree. Few other climbers will give such a good account of themselves in really shady places and its spectacular, lacecap heads of white flowers appear all the more startling in such situations. It may need artificial support at first, but once its aerial roots start to grow, it rapidly establishes itself as a most valuable plant for gardening in depth.*

The hydrangea for tiny gardens is undoubtedly the dwarf, red-flowered 'Pia'. This is no more than 60cm/24in tall and its flowers last well into the late autumn and early winter, when they change to deep purple. It is a congenial plant that looks right when surrounded by low-growing neighbors; *Alchemilla mollis*, whose soft, gray-green leaves hold droplets of water on their surfaces after rain like bright diamonds, is ideal. One or two Hart's-tongue Ferns planted nearby would be perfect.

In large gardens, even the biggest lacecaps can be planted in drifts among trees, where they will provide interest almost all the year round and strike a note of woodland tranquility. However, for those whose gardens have no pretensions to woodland, the amazingly variegated 'Quadricolor' is small enough to fit, and three plants in a group will greatly add to the all-seasons appeal of the garden. The leaves are strikingly but coolly variegated in green, gray, cream and gold. The gold occurs at the leaf margins on plants that are well grown and fed; on poorly grown plants the gold does not happen and this is why the varietal name 'Tricolor' is sometimes met with. The variety does not exist.

The blue color in hydrangeas is a matter of choosing blue-flowered varieties and growing them in acid soils in which there is a supply of free aluminum. On really alkaline soils it is best to stick to pinks or reds ('Quadricolor' is a pink lacecap). If your soil is acid but the blues are disappointing, a two-weekly dose of blueing compound or alum crystals to the soil should correct matters.

Hydrangeas are very tolerant of maritime exposures, and can be grown as hedges if you have room or need. There is no better flower for cutting, especially after the flowers have changed their texture in autumn, and it is fun to be able to walk along, choosing as you go a few heads of flowers for your autumn arrangement. That they started flowering in the height of summer will add piquancy and a little nostalgia for the colorful season that has now passed.

ABOVE *Mophead hydrangeas have ball-like inflorescences. H. 'Vibraye' is one of the earliest to flower and, on a suitable soil, is one of the bluest. It will flower for much of the summer and into the autumn, after which many of the flower heads will over-winter as green-turquoise.*

LEFT *The lacecap form of hydrangea inflorescence is admirably illustrated by H. 'Quadricolor', a pink-flowered variety, whose foliage is among the best of all variegated plants.*

83

AUTUMN

*Hazy autumn has shining fruits among mellow colors and late,
long-lasting flowers defying the advent of frost.*

AUTUMN STARTS WHEN CHILL airs hint that the downturn of the year is beginning. There may be a touch of wine-red in the leaves of *Liquidambar* trees but there is as yet no real indication of the approaching leaf fall. Woody plants have spent some time ripening their growths in the summer heat and they will continue this process for a while yet, and some of them still have their flowering period to come. But above all, autumn is a period of transition – late summer merging into early winter through the medium of one of the most poignantly beautiful times, whose effects are often intensely dramatic.

Flowering shrubs

Many summer-flowering shrubs carry on well into autumn and these go to provide a fairly large element of late color in the garden. Some shrubs do, though, have their main flowering period at this time, but they are relatively few in number. It is not hard to see why – there is little time for seed to be set and pollinating insects are much fewer once the first frosts have arrived.

Summer into autumn

Hardy fuchsias play a very large part in the autumn garden although they start flowering in summer. It is only in very cold inland areas that these cannot be grown. Give them the faintest smell of the sea and they will withstand heavy frosts and icy winds, even if they are cut down to the ground by them. Their out-of-flower qualities are few, but their season of bloom is so long that they have an important role in the all-seasons garden, and particularly in autumn. Two good examples are *Fuchsia magellanica* 'Riccartonii', a large shrub furnished to the ground with neat foliage and masses of small purple-and-red dangling flowers, and *F.m.* var. *gracilis*, which is on a smaller scale with larger, slimmer flowers.

Where the climate allows, you can use fuchsias as colorful hedges. They make ideal filterers of the wind and can become effective boundaries between different garden elements, such as the vegetable and flower garden. Such a hedge will have an immensely long flowering season if you plant it with the spring-flowering *Clematis alpina*, *C. macropetala* (both blue) and *C. montana*.

If you are looking for a neighbor for fuchsias, you should consider the yuccas. These exotic-looking shrubs, with their tropical appearance and bold, strap-shaped, pointed leaves, bear their huge panicles of creamy flowers in late summer and early autumn and they make an exciting contrast with the fuchsias, both when in and out of flower. Yuccas are unexpectedly hardy, particularly *Yucca recurviflora* and the even more spectacular *Y. gloriosa*, and will stand a lot of frost. However, they do not like snow, especially snow in drifts.

RIGHT *The very essence of autumn: Japanese Maples glow in shades of red and gold above a green carpet of ferns. A touch of yellow is provided by the small shrub Fothergilla gardenii. This quiet corner of a larger garden is ablaze with color, though an evergreen background ensures no lack of interest when the deciduous leaves have fallen.*

Autumn flowers
Fuchsia magellanica 'Alba' *dangles delicately colored flowers below its neat leaves for months. Hypericum 'Hidcote' is easy to grow and has a long succession of flowers. Yucca recurviflora gives the garden a tropical air, and has huge towers of white blooms.*

Fuchsia magellanica 'Alba'

Hypericum 'Hidcote'

Yucca recurviflora

Seasonal flower color

Yellow is an uncommon color after the late spring – certainly among shrubs – so late-blooming, yellow-flowered shrubs have an added value in the garden because they are reminiscent of spring. Given this, and their long flowering period, the hypericums can be found space in gardens of all sizes.

Hypericum 'Hidcote' is a compact shrub of about 1.5m/5ft in height and it produces its large, saucer-shaped flowers with great generosity. They are of a bright, buttery yellow, which shows up to great effect from a distance. Its best position is in full sun among other shrubs, where its flowers can be easily seen but where its lower part, which is not particularly attractive, can be hidden. It is extremely hardy, more so than the even better *H.* 'Rowallane', whose color is a rich gold and whose flowers are even larger. *H.* × *moseranum* 'Tricolor' is a completely prostrate plant with 7cm/2½in flowers over foliage that is variegated with white and pink. Several in a sheltered spot make first-class ground cover.

A marvelous succession of colors is provided by the late-flowering *Clerodendrum trichotomum*. The flowers are white and highly scented and are surrounded by maroon calyxes. These persist to surround fruits whose color is unique among hardy shrubs and trees – a turquoise tone that tends toward blue. The variety *C.t.* var. *fargesii* fruits much more freely than the type.

Perhaps the most exotic seasonal color is provided by the hardy hibiscus. These forms of *Hibiscus syriacus* are among the most lovely of autumn-flowering shrubs, and you need to place them carefully in order to appreciate their colors without those colors conflicting with others. Their large mallowlike flowers in shades of purple-red, purple-blue and white (there is always a blotching of purple or maroon) are their great glory, but they are best seen among foliage of a kind that presents an appropriately exotic appearance. *Fatsia japonica* has ideal large, palmate, subtropical-looking leaves, but the large paddles of a magnolia will do just as well.

H. syriacus 'Diane' is not a large shrub and it will fit well into the smallest garden, but it should have this foliage accompaniment – preferably evergreen – since it is not a plant of great beauty when out of flower. This pure white sterile form will continue blooming until frost.

Coastal windbreaks

One of the most difficult problems in gardening is posed by wind in coastal gardens. Luckily, the sea has a moderating influence on temperature, so the fact that most of the best plants for windbreaks are slightly tender need not necessarily be a drawback. It is also to their credit that many of them are shrubs that flower in the autumn – the time when storms are at their fiercest. Fuchsias and hydrangeas (see pp. 83 and 86) have already been mentioned as being tolerant of maritime exposure; two other genera are *Escallonia* and *Tamarix*.

Escallonias are untidy plants inland and their white, pink or red flowers tend to be sparsely scattered. Near to the coast, however, they grow much more compactly and become almost covered in bloom. Their evergreen foliage is neat

ABOVE *The colorful berries of* Clerodendrum trichotomum, *with their persistent red calyxes, present a most unusual autumn picture. The shrub has white flowers, which occur in late summer and are powerfully fragrant.*

RIGHT *In this autumn garden, heathers play an important role in a well-planted scene full of contrasts of form. The tiny massed foliage of the heathers is in direct opposition to the bold, broad leaves of the bergenias, while the sentinel evergreen conifers stand out sharply against their deciduous background.*

and glossy and provides an effective background of dark green on the landward side.

Tamarisks are tall, feathery plants that look absolutely at home by the sea, although they will grow almost anywhere in sun. They will establish on sand or shingle and do not require a rich or well-fed soil. *Tamarisk pentandra* has lovely rose-pink flowers in autumn. By selecting a variety of species it is possible to have a shelterbelt of tamarisks in flower from the spring through to the late autumn, and their leafless branches in winter are not stark but more like woody fennel or asparagus.

Heathers

The lovely heaths and heathers continue with the myriad of varieties of *Calluna vulgaris*. Their flowering period spans the whole of the season, having started in late summer, and the tremendous variation in foliage color – and plant shapes and sizes – makes them one of the great features of the autumn garden. *Calluna* is a lime-hater, but it has shallow roots and so can be grown in soils that have been made of peat and sand and laid to a sufficient depth over existing limy soils.

There can be few genera that contribute so much to the year-round beauty of the garden. While they are, above all, to be planted *en masse*, each individual sprig of neat, even foliage and flowers repays careful appreciation. When planted so that the golds complement the greens, and the grays lend a somber contrast to the orange and red of examples such as 'Robert Chapman', their overall effect is wonderfully eye-filling but by no means dazzling.

Other plants can be grown among the heathers, particularly such plants as *Vaccinium myrtillus*, whose black, edible 'bilberries' appear in the autumn. The bright, blue flowers of *Ceratostigma willmottianum*, planted on higher, drier ground of the heath and heather garden will introduce a new color. Dwarf pines, such as *Pinus sylvestris* 'Beuvronensis' or *P. mugo* 'Mops' might be among its neighbors, too.

Autumn foliage color

How much color the dying leaves of deciduous trees and shrubs will give depends on the weather of the current year, the climate of your region and the plants you have chosen to grow. The duration of the color will depend upon the frequency and the strength of the wind – a strong gale can reduce a tree full of late leaf to a skeleton of bare branches in a single day. Because of these variables, a good year for autumn color is something to be truly savored. In general, though, a sharp contrast between summer heat and winter cold makes for the best color, but some plants can always be relied on to perform well.

From the all-seasons point of view, this colorful period covers only a small part of the year, and so it would be a mistake to choose a plant solely for autumn foliage color. This characteristic should always be taken as a bonus over and above the qualities that are going to make that plant a welcome addition to the garden during the rest of the year.

Nyssa sylvatica, *the Tupelo Tree from North America (above), is one of the best small-to-medium-sized trees for reliable autumn color. Its foliage tones can be spectacular, varying from rich gold, through orange to red.*

Sorbus 'Embley', *right, has the best autumn color among the Mountain Ashes and retains its leaves longer than most. It is a neat tree, suitable for small gardens. Its color is accentuated when it can be seen against a dark background, and particularly if this can be achieved so that the sun can strike through the red leaves.*

Acer palmatum 'Heptalo-
bum Osakazuki' *(above) has
the most brilliantly colored
foliage of all the Japanese
Maples. Enkianthus
campanulatus (above right)
has beautiful, subtly colored,
sulfur bronze flowers in
spring, and in autumn
becomes a flaming landmark.
Liquidambar styraciflua
(right) begins to change
color before most other trees,
showing an occasional vivid
red among its leaves (below),
which have very subtle
shades and patterns.*

Accentuating autumn color

There are many ways in which you can appreciate and use autumn foliage in your garden – by having dark backgrounds, for example, or by taking advantage of the translucent qualities of the leaves and the beautiful effect created when sunlight shines through them. It is a complete waste if leaves can be seen only in silhouette against the sky, since then they will appear black. You should lose no opportunity of making autumn foliage a feature of reflections in water, especially since, at this time of year, evenings tend to be still and the surface of water becomes mirrorlike in quality. It is in such still and tranquil late afternoons that the color of the dying leaves, most outstandingly the reds, can be seen to have the most dramatic effect. If the day has been clear and the sun has just begun to set and is no longer shining into the garden, have a close look at a plant like a deciduous azalea or *Euonymus alatus* when its foliage is at its reddest. If the light is right you will become aware of the most intense and mesmerizing dazzle, but one that has no discomfort in it at all.

Euonymus includes some of the very best species for late autumn color, and these usually have conspicuous red seeds hanging from their capsules, or the capsules themselves may be red. *E. oxyphyllus* has colored capsules and its leaves turn from fresh green to a gorgeous mixture of red and purple. *E. grandiflorus* grows to about 3.5m/12ft and it has yellow flowers and yellow capsules with red seeds. The combination of these with deep wine-colored autumn foliage is superb.

In the taller background population of the garden the Smoke Tree *Cotinus coggygria* (formerly *Rhus cotinus*) is a large shrub that earns its place through its flowers, which are carried in large, tan-colored inflorescences that turn smoke-gray later in the summer and persist into autumn when the leaves become orange-gold. The effect is just like smoke, and in the variety *purpureus* it appears pink and gives rise to the name "Burning Bush". 'Flame' is a cultivar whose autumn foliage is brilliant orange, verging on red. The most brightly colored cotinus of all is a different species, *C. obovatus*, which is a larger shrub altogether. They all look best planted among other large plants and so that their puffs of 'smoke' appear as if coming from behind other things, but they should also be seen with the sun on them.

A lawn is an excellent place to grow trees – such as the fastigiate Mountain Ashes – that have good form as well as autumn foliage. The upright Mountain Ash, *Sorbus* 'Joseph Rock', will display its amber fruits to best advantage as a lawn specimen, and the various shades of red, orange and purple in its many leafleted leaves will show up well.

An autumn comparison
Color and grandeur are constant themes in this large garden, but as the seasons change so does the focus of attention and the atmosphere. In spring (above) the brightly colored blooms of the evergreen azaleas glow against a backdrop of green. In autumn (right) the balance is totally transformed. Instead of being the active partner in the scene, the bank of azaleas assumes the passive role, as its neat, rounded shapes and rich, dark-green tones become, in their turn, the foil for the flamboyance of the brilliant leaf colors of the Tupelo Trees (Nyssa sylvatica).

Small trees for the garden

Autumn color is not the prerogative of large gardens. It is true that if you have such a garden you can give full rein to the staggering effects that autumn can provide. In the small garden, though, it is all a matter of scale. It is possible, for example, to reduce the garden to the size of a trough and still have color. The tiny Mountain Ash *Sorbus reducta* will seldom exceed 30cm/12in in height, and its pinnate leaves turn to beautiful shades of red and purple, while its fruits are white with a pink flush.

On lime-free soils the deciduous azaleas provide rich reds, while *Fothergilla gardenii* will display bright gold on a shrub only 90cm/36in or so high. A garden of around 95 sq m/1,000 sq ft is quite big enough for one of the larger species of *Sorbus* that fall into the Mountain Ash, or Aucuparia, group, as well as that marvelous all-seasons tree *Amelanchier lamarckii*. This tree has abundant racemes of white flowers in spring, when the young foliage is copper-red, and it is one of the most richly colored of all small trees in autumn. What is more, it is an easy and adaptable tree and it will grow in any good garden soil.

The Japanese Maples are outstanding among the smaller autumn-flowering trees and shrubs. The species is *Acer palmatum* and it is extremely variable in its forms as well as in the colors of its autumn leaves. The very best colors tend to occur in the Heptalobum group, which have reasonably large leaves with seven lobes instead of the usual five and are ideal for small gardens. 'Heptalobum Lutescens' turns a rich, buttery gold, while 'Osakazuki' takes on tones of brilliant scarlet. The Coral Bark Maple, A. 'Senkaki' becomes the color of a canary's plumage and when it has lost its leaves it is one of the best trees for winter bark color.

Almost as good as 'Senkaki' is A. *capillipes*. This is a small tree belonging to the group known as 'Snakebark' Maples, whose bark is striated and striped like the skin of a green snake. A. *ginnala* is a small tree with three-lobed leaves that turn to a beautiful red. They do not, however, stay long on the trees in this state, but the tree is well worth including because its white flowers are conspicuous in spring and they have an extremely pleasing fragrance. The taller maples are superb when you can see them at a distance against a really dark background.

The importance of form in a plant is well shown by this comparison of Acer palmatum 'Dissectum' in autumn and in winter. Although totally different in their effects, the autumn foliage and the winter snow bring out the beautiful shape of the tree to the extent that there is little difference, if any, in its beauty in either season.

The greens of foliage, grass and moss are the backcloth against which all garden colors are best displayed. In this sunlit garden, the jewel-like colors of autumn are made the more intense by being seen in a predominantly green environment. The effects of light can be made vividly dramatic, especially in autumn, and it is a good idea always to have in mind the places where the sun will strike at different times of the year. A sliver of sunshine along a tree trunk and the glitter of sunlight through autumn leaves make for unforgettably delicious moments.

Berries, like flowers and
autumn foliage, benefit
greatly by being seen against
a background of green.
Evergreen foliage plays a
vital role in the garden in all
the seasons; in this garden it
is playing several parts. The
distinct shapes of the
evergreens lend structure and
character to a corner of the
garden, while they act in
contrast to the grays and early
autumn foliage around them.
The red berries, though, are
displayed brightly against the
dark evergreens in a way that
can be achieved readily in
almost any garden. Trees and
shrubs will remain decorated
with bright fruits longer if
they are placed, as here, near
a garden path, where the
birds that might take them
will be disturbed more often.

Autumn fruits

In the 'Season of mists and mellow fruitfulness' we could perhaps do without the mists but not without the fruits. Generally, we think of fruits in terms of the edible varieties, but the all-seasons gardener includes all those seed vessels that are botanically fruits and attractive to look at. Thus, the bitter crab apple is as important as the big, juicy eating apple, and the Japanese Quince claims our attention as much as the culinary pear does.

Japanese Quinces are now all included in *Chaenomeles*, where once they were *Cydonia*. Gardeners have a habit of referring to them as 'Japonicas' although there are many species of plants with the specific epithet *japonica*, which simply means 'from Japan'. *C. japonica* is a fairly dwarf shrub of considerable garden merit, which has the habit of covering itself completely with bright red flowers in spring. It also bears small fruits, which are red on the side where the sun strikes them and yellow where it does not. Most other garden forms of Japanese Quinces are varieties of *C. speciosa*; they have large flowers in pink, crimson or blood red and they may be seen as early as the late winter. The main flowering period, however, is in the spring, but it can continue into the early summer. In autumn, the fruits are about 2.5 to 5cm/1 to 2in across, yellow in color with small speckles. These fruits are edible, but bitter in their raw state, and are best used for making jelly.

Japanese Quinces have many uses in the garden, although they are most often seen as decoration for sunny walls, where they certainly flower magnificently. However, one large specimen growing as a freestanding lawn shrub can be a lovely and an unusual sight or, for a different effect, several can make a fine hedge. They will tolerate a lot of pruning, which should be carried out in the summer, so they are not difficult to shape. They need sun though; planted in the shade, they lose their all-seasons qualities and become mere spring bloomers.

Hips and berries

By growing shrub and species roses you have the benefit of their fruits in autumn, at least until the birds get among them. Among the best fruiting roses are the varieties of *Rosa rugosa*, whose hips are bright red and shaped something like small tomatoes. With large, scented flowers produced over a long period and foliage that is not only attractive but scented in its own right, these are very much all-seasons plants.

LEFT *The Rugosa Rose 'Fru Dagmar Hastrup' is a compact, bushy shrub with clear pink, fragrant flowers in summer. The large, tomato-like fruits are darker red than in most rugosas.*

BELOW *In autumn, the glistening red hips of* Rosa virginiana *are borne on a shrub whose glossy green leaves have turned orange-red, crimson and then yellow.*

Rose hips vary in size and shape almost endlessly, from the enormous, flagon-shaped ones of *R. moyesii* to the massed tiny ones of *R. filipes*. They can be brilliant, sealing-wax red, orange or almost brown and they are always lovely, perhaps never more so than in *R. nitida* when startlingly red, bristly fruits are matched by its wonderful autumn foliage. By growing these plants among other shrubs, you can guarantee that for a short while they will blaze out from among their neighbors in just as dramatic a manner as anything in flower.

Berries, of course, are a feature and a delight at this time of year. The most worthy of specimens for the all-seasons garden retain their pretty crop well into the winter months, and these are dealt with in detail on pages 115-19.

Conifers

Although the chief contribution of the conifers is made by their foliage and form, some of the most subtle notes of autumn are provided by their fruits, those magnificent cones that give them their name.

The Silver Firs belong to the genus *Abies*, one of the more noteworthy characteristics of which is the way in which the cones stand erect on the upper sides of the branches. In many species they are blue, purple or black, and in *A. koreana* the cones are not only extremely attractive but they are borne on a tree that is of an ideal shape

and size for the smaller garden. In a genus that includes some very tall trees, it is notably small, attaining at most a height of just over 10.5m/35ft after many years. When it is only 90cm/36in tall, however, it will start bearing cones of a bright violet-purple, about 7.5cm/3in high and 2.5cm/1in thick. It is a plant that is a delight to come across as a surprise, and a good place to plant it is where a lawn curves to form an alcove among such things as bamboos. In the center of such a small patch of grass its presence is felt in a way that is lost in a more open situation.

Another good fir, *A. delavayi*, is larger, making a medium-sized tree. Its cones can reach a length of about 10cm/4in and they are very dark violet with a lot of blue mixed in.

Among the pines, *Pinus wallichiana* has perhaps the most amazing cones of all. They are cylindrical, pendulous and an astonishing 25cm/10in long. The tree itself is most attractive when young, but you need to shelter it from wind damage to prevent its looking tatty at a later stage. Plant this tree on its own so that it will remain clothed to the ground with branches and long, drooping foliage.

In total contrast to the large, woody cones of the pines, the 'fruits' of the yew do not look as though they belong to a conifer at all. The bright red, fleshy berries are always attractive, but the yellow ones of *Taxus baccata* 'Lutea' are unexpectedly striking.

RIGHT A range of conifers — a mixture of tall, small, conical and spreading ones — creates a telling effect in this garden. Their multiplicity of shapes and sizes have been used to create a pleasant framework for a garden that looks just as good in autumn as in any other season. (It is shown in winter on page 109.) However a garden with too many conifers becomes gloomy if they are tall, and too much like a collection of oddities if they are dwarf. The great variety that is available should be used, as here, with lighter, more airy plants that will create movement and to give a background structure and a coherence to the garden when herbaceous plants have retired from the scene. Here, the balance between evergreen and deciduous has been very finely struck.

Abies koreana

Pinus wallichiana

Cones
The violet-purple color of the cones of Abies koreana is most unusual and a strong contrast to the dark green foliage. The attractive curved, hanging cones of Pinus wallichiana are borne from early in the life of the tree.

Autumn bulbs

The autumn-flowering bulbs are far less well-known than the spring ones, perhaps with the exception of *Cyclamen hederifolium* (formerly, *C. neapolitanum*). This reliable little plant flowers in the early autumn before its leaves appear and it can be obtained in both pink and white forms. As with many bulbs, this is a plant for setting in drifts and the ideal places are in the shade of evergreen trees and around and among shrubs.

Where the sun strikes the ground around shrubs, and it is warm and a little more open, is where *Leucojum autumnale*, the Autumn Snowflake, likes to display its white, pink-tinged bells, at about the same time as the cyclamen is flowering in the more shady spots.

The genus *Crocus* includes several autumn species, but the term 'Autumn Crocus' is usually used to refer to *Colchicum*, which is not a crocus at all. Colchicums have flowers that appear before the leaves and they are shaped like slim-stemmed goblets in pink, in pink-purple or in white. Of the true crocuses, the best and most easy to grow is *Crocus speciosus*. Its appearance is not unlike that of the colchicum, but the color range is different – from deep mauve to a light gray-blue or white – and the leaves are much slimmer. It prefers a little more light than a colchicum does, but is, nevertheless, perfectly suitable for planting among shrubs or small herbaceous plants. *Crocus cancellatus* is later to flower and it has larger blooms, usually of a pale silver color with a yellow throat. *C. sativus* is the plant from which saffron is obtained and it is a beautiful garden plant.

The nerines are possibly the most beautiful of all the bulbs that can be seen at this time of the year. The easiest one to grow is *Nerine bowdenii* and it is certainly the hardiest, surviving temperatures down to 14°F/−10°C. Its flowers are held in clusters of six or eight and they are among the finest gems of the plant world. They are star-shaped and each segment is wavy and recurved at the end. The color is of an amazing

ABOVE *Although not true crocuses, members of the genus* Colchicum *are known as Autumn Crocuses. Their goblet-shaped flowers look neat and pretty in the autumn sunshine.*

LEFT Galanthus nivalis reginae-olgae, *a subspecies of the early spring snowdrop, flowers in the autumn before its leaves are formed. It should be grown where it can be kept fairly dry in summer.*

sugared pink, and the result is an iridescence that is like nothing else. *N. bowdenii* flowers best when its bulbs are crowded. Although it will flower in its first year after planting, it will often wait for three or more years before giving of its best. If you have a sunny wall, then the frosted pink of the flowers will look wonderful against the gray of an old wall or the warm brown of sandstone.

Schizostylis coccinea is not strictly speaking a bulb, but in gardening terms it might as well be. The flowers are again star-shaped but they are not undulating and twisted as are those of nerines. They vary from rose-pink to scarlet and the form 'Major' is larger in all its parts. The border is the place for *S. coccinea* and it is seen to better advantage among herbaceous plants than around shrubs.

ABOVE LEFT Schizostylis coccinea 'Rose Glow', *is a light pink variety of a valuable, late autumn-flowering plant ranging from this color to scarlet.*

ABOVE *The flowers of* Cyclamen hederifolium *begin to appear before the leaves, which are always beautifully marked and persist until the following summer.*

LEFT *The incomparable sugar-pink of* Nerine bowdenii *and its unique flower shape make it a most desirable addition to the autumn garden.*

Climbers

Although the main season for *Clematis* ends with the summer, there are still several that reserve their main display for autumn. 'Ernest Markham' starts flowering in late summer and keeps going almost to leaf-fall. Its maroon-red flowers are particularly effective when seen against the golden late foliage of, for example, a corylopsis. Even later flowering are 'Madame Baron Veillard', which has medium-sized rose-colored blooms with lilac tints, and 'Lady Betty Balfour', whose flowers are purple and extremely large.

Among the *Clematis* species are plants with great autumn effect, some of which are really rampant climbers. *C. serratifolia* has yellow flowers, which are small, but carried in profusion. It is unmistakable because of its conspicuous anthers, which are a rich shade somewhere between red and purple, and because of its seed heads in which the filaments are 5cm/2in long and give the appearance of bunches of coarse cotton. *C. orientalis* is closely related to it. It has larger flowers of a deeper shade of yellow, the sepals of which look a little like orange-peel. Even better is *C. tangutica*, whose flowers are similar but of an even solider color and have sepals which are up to 5cm/2in long. All have the same sort of attractive seed heads, which are almost as valuable in the garden as the flowers and with which they are often mixed in the latter part of the season.

Akebia quinata, apart from being an attractive plant, is also an oddity. It is a vigorous, twining climber with good-looking leaves divided into five oval leaflets. If it is grown up a pergola or into a suitable small tree near a path, it will present its unusually shaped, small, purple flowers at just the right level for their fragrance to be appreciated in the spring. It is what happens later that is odd. As you walk beneath the plant in autumn you will see what look like big, mauve-blue sausages that seem as if they have no connection with the plant kingdom whatever.

All is revealed later on when the 'sausages' split to reveal rows of black seed set in pastelike jelly.

Among the vines there are two that can claim space in the all-seasons garden. *Vitis* 'Brant' will decorate a large pergola or other suitable support with large, lobed leaves that turn dark red in autumn. The vine produces grapes, too, which are aromatic and fairly sweet to taste. Large trees can comfortably play host to *Vitis coignetiae*. The leaves of this climber are 30cm/12in across and of a lobed heart shape, green on top and rustily furry underneath. The intense richness of the scarlet and crimson shades that these huge leaves develop in autumn is an extremely fine sight, especially when the vine is allowed to grow up and into a deciduous tree whose foliage turns yellow.

RIGHT *The long shadows and clear, crisp light of autumn provide marvelous visual effects, picking out the structures of stems, leaves and seed heads in silhouette. A crowded herbaceous planting is given structure by strongly sculptured evergreens, whose presence will become even more marked as winter approaches.*

BELOW *The silky seed heads and lemon-peel flowers of* Clematis tangutica *occur together in autumn. The divided leaves are attractive as well, and this hardy plant is an excellent climber.*

Herbaceous plants

The garden scene in autumn benefits greatly from many of the summer-flowering herbaceous perennials that carry on well past their main season of bloom – some of the Red-hot Pokers (*Kniphofia*), for example, may keep on flowering into early autumn. The selection known as 'Bressingham Strain' will successfully bridge the seasons from summer into autumn. There is something of the hot-country ethos about them, and they need the company of plants of a similar nature, such as yuccas, and plenty of sun.

In contrast, because they are plants from much cooler places, are those truly autumn flowerers, the Japanese Anemones. There are many varieties of *Anemone japonica*, and few can beat the white ones for open spaces among shrubs or beneath trees. *A.j.* 'Alba' has large white flowers on stems that, like the other varieties, are 90cm/36in high and it never fails to provide a riotous tumble of light in shady places. 'September Charm' keeps on with its 15cm/6in, pink blooms right through the autumn. For best effect, plant this, and the almost double 'Lady Gilmour', among evergreen shrubs that have finished flowering. It looks best if the shrubs are taller than the anemones, which should be planted in large groups.

Astrantia 'Margery Fish' remains in flower for as much as two months later than does the species *A. major*, which is more usually grown. It is 15cm/6in or so taller than the Japanese Anemones and likes the same sort of places to grow in, where it will produce a long succession of shaggy heads of small white flowers. Both the astrantias and the anemones spread by underground rhizomes and large colonies can be built up in time. Take care, however, to keep the ground free from bits of rotten twig that may fall from surrounding trees, since both plants are quickly infected with honey fungus.

Asters have a late and long period for flowering, and these plants are often stiff and susceptible to disease. However, one, *Aster*

Autumn is a season of tranquility and a time for reflection. Although its apogee is short-lived, it is such a richly rewarding time that every effort should be made to plan for it in the garden. Mosses, ferns, and plants of the woodland floor are redolent of peacefulness, and it will be a pleasant and rewarding experience to take a gentle stroll round a garden such as this, where strong, fleeting autumn color is in harmony with quiet, moist greenness.

×*frikartii*, is uniquely natural-looking and is possessed of great elegance. Its lavender-blue daisies do not belong in the usual sort of formal border but in among the more aristocratic of the smaller shrubs, especially those with gray leaves. *Rosa rubrifolia*, whose grayness is tinged with hints of dark crimson, has a stillness in the wind against which the blue flowers can dance. *Elaeagnus macrophylla*, whose silver color needs no distraction early in the year, will have faded to gray-green, and it now benefits from the airiness of the aster while itself lending fragrance from its own rather inconspicuous flowers.

It would not be a good idea to grow the aster where Candelabra Primulas gave their color earlier in the year, as it would swamp them completely, but you can grow astrantias and Japanese Anemones with primulas, provided that they are lifted and divided every couple of years before they have a chance to overgrow the primulas. This is not really worth the trouble in larger gardens but in small ones, where space has to be used to best advantage, it is an excellent way of maximizing the all-seasons appeal of a small patch of ground.

Although really a shrub, the Cape Fuchsia *Phygelius capensis* must be treated as a herbaceous perennial where there is frost. This is not really a fuchsia at all, but its tubular, light red flowers are similar to those of some species of fuchsia. It is a beautiful plant and it flowers from just after midsummer to midautumn. Its near-relative *P. aequalis* 'Yellow Trumpet' is even more attractive, with foliage of a light lettuce green and flowers that are long, tubular and light cream yellow. It starts flowering in midsummer and just keeps on going.

Summer flowers in winter

Salvia is a huge genus that includes herbaceous plants as well as shrubs and several with thick, woody stems that are cut to the ground every winter by severe frost. They will shoot from the base again the next year and flower with great abandon. While none of them is really hardy,

they will grow happily in open gardens that experience temperatures down to 14°F/−10°C provided that the frosts are not prolonged. There are three species of true distinction in the genus and the tallest and most spectacularly beautiful of these is *Salvia concolor*. It will attain 3m/10ft in height from scratch in one season. As well as producing large, heart-shaped, velvety leaves, throughout the whole of autumn you will witness a staggering show of clear, dark-sky-blue flowers in long spikes. *S. ambigens* is darker blue and about 1.2m/4ft high, while *S. rutilans* has apple-green foliage that smells of pineapples and a long succession of bright rose-pink flowers of the characteristic lipped shape of the genus. While in colder areas they will flower until the end of autumn, and should then be cut down and protected, in extremely mild areas of the Northern Hemisphere, the three can be seen in flower on Christmas Day.

The Cape Fuchsia, Phygelius capensis, *can grow to a considerable height in very mild gardens, but is usually seen as a low-growing, very floriferous plant with a burst of flowering in autumn.*

WINTER

*There is color and substance even in winter, though familiar plants
sometimes appear in new guises, picked out in frost or dressed in snow.*

W INTER, FOR THE all-seasons gardener, is a period of only about two months, when everything comes to a standstill and there is almost no change going on. Although little may be happening in the winter garden for this short time, this is all the more reason why it should be made to look as interesting as possible, particularly as you are likely to spend much time wistfully looking at it from indoors.

Form

Form is everything in winter. Ugly plants will stick out like sore thumbs and, similarly, well-shaped, elegant, or nicely colored ones will become prominent. Plant associations take on an even greater importance, and the play of the different shades of green will catch the eye in the near-absence of flower color.

There may be periods when snow will lie and you should take some pains to see that the plants will give a good account of themselves in their task of standing out from the white blanket in good order. The attractive and architectural qualities of the skeletons of deciduous plants will be revealed, and this is above all where colored stems and trunks come into play, although they are vitally important during the whole season.

Evergreens

Evergreen trees and shrubs are of the utmost importance in providing structure and constant appeal in an all-seasons garden, and this is particularly so in winter. Once herbaceous plants have died down and deciduous trees and shrubs shed their leaves, the garden would be bare without the presence of evergreens to give it substance. Color is important in the winter garden – as in the other seasons – but winter flowers and berries need to be seen against an evergreen background – and indeed many of the best winter-flowering and berrying plants are, as we shall see, evergreen.

Conifers

Conifers can be planted for great winter effect. Few kinds of plants have such definitely stated shapes or make such strong contrasts, one with another. For this reason they can be tremendously effective planted in groups. Among such a group the tall column of the dark green *Chamaecyparis lawsoniana* 'Kilmacurragh' will be a contrasting background both in color and shape to *C.l.* 'Pembury Blue', which is perhaps only half as tall and is of a pyramidal shape and silver-blue in color. *Cupressus sempervirens*, another tall, dark green column, can stand sentinel alongside 'Kilmacurragh', while in front of it *Picea brewerana* 'Brewer's Weeping Spruce' introduces a conical shape. Stand *Chamaecyparis* 'Golden King' at one side and this will echo the cone-shape of the picea with the introduction of gold foliage, while in the angle these make you can provide an arrangement of colors and shapes of the slow-growing conifers, in sizes down to the dwarfs.

RIGHT *The beauty of this garden in winter owes a great deal to the diversity of form, which the frost enhances. The shapes and sizes of the evergreens complement each other and contrast strongly with the stark outlines of the deciduous trees. There is no concession to untidiness; untrimmed lawn edges and forgotten flower stems would have spoiled the scene. (This garden is shown in detail on p. 99.)*

Conifer shapes
There is a vast range of shapes, colors and sizes of conifers; some examples are shown below. Carefully and selectively chosen to contrast and complement each other they can play an important role in the all-seasons garden.

Cupressus sempervirens   *Picea engelmanii* var. *glauca*

Picea pungens 'Globosa'

Abies nordmanniana 'Golden spreader'

Stems

It is worth emphasizing again and again that the stems and branches of trees and shrubs should receive as much attention when they are being chosen as any other aspect of the plants. Red and yellow *Cornus* stems, the pale blue trunks of *Eucalyptus* and willows, the shaggy peeling, mahogany bark of *Stuartia*, standing out of the snow or with a touch of hoar frost glistening here and there in sunlight as it penetrates a winter mist, conjure up a winter scene of great beauty and mystery.

The white, ghostly trunk and branches of the Snow Gum, Eucalyptus pauciflora ssp. niphophila (left), are an outstanding feature at all times of the year, but especially in winter. In complete contrast, thickets of stems, such as those of Cornus alba 'Sibirica' or Salix 'Britzensis' (above left) bring bright color to the winter scene, and a warm glow is added by the honey tones of the trunk of Prunus maackii (above). A very striking effect is provided by the pale, papery, peeling bark of the Himalayan birch, Betula utilis (above middle).

Hardy perennials

The forms of hardy perennials also take on special significance in winter. Strong shapes are what is needed, along with a certain rigidity of structure. Long grass can look chilly being tugged this way and that by the wind. It should be cut down and the herbaceous plants tidied up. What may well remain are, for example, the huge swordlike leaves of the phormiums (New Zealand Flaxes), growing in large clumps of sabers and lending a warming air of the subtropics instead of a hint of the polar regions. *Phormium tenax* has a variety with purple leaves about 1.8m/6ft high and also a tall variegated form. *P. cookianum*, about half the size of *P. tenax*, has a good form called 'Tricolor' and a first-class variety called 'Yellow Wave', whose leaves are striped in gold and light green.

The yuccas perform a similar service, and they will strike an even warmer note when planted with *Cordyline australis*, the New Zealand 'Cabbage Palm', a member of the Lily family with a woody, pithy stem that can attain the height and thickness of a short, stout tree. Both these genera will grow in temperate gardens, as they stand much more cold than is often expected of them, but they will not tolerate prolonged frosts and are plants for maritime areas where the sea moderates the winters.

Not every plant makes you feel chilly when it is blown about. *Arundinaria nitida* is a neat bamboo, whose canes rise to about 2m/6ft before arching over in a most graceful manner. The play of breezes over it produces a very peaceful effect and it can look magical with frost on the stems. It is an ideal plant for the waterside, where tranquility should be the keynote.

Flowers in the winter garden

In saying, as I did, that winter is the season when there is almost no change occurring, the emphasis is on the 'almost', as there is a thread that runs through the garden as a link between autumn and spring; a thread that, except per-haps in the coldest gardens, bursts into life here and there and shows itself in flowers and in the slow swelling of buds.

Foliage and flowers

Mahonias would be worthy of a place in the garden for their form and evergreen foliage alone even if they did not flower, and the winter-flowering species are truly magnificent plants. Their very bold, stiff, spiny, pinnate foliage is so striking that much thought should go into their placing; it is a good idea to make a feature of a group of them where they can be seen to good advantage at winter time. They all do well in any fertile soil and are happy growing over limestone.

Mahonia japonica is an extremely beautiful plant with leaves over 30cm/12in, each with numerous leaflets. The racemes of yellow flowers are low and fragrant, and each cluster curves so as to be almost pendulous. Whereas M. *japonica* is hardy, the even more imposing M. *lomariifolia* is less so, although it will stand severe frosts of relatively short duration. It is a large shrub of very upright habit and its 60cm/24in leaves are furnished with nineteen narrow

Mahonias
Mahonia japonica *has 13-19 leaflets on each leaf, and its racemes of flowers spread sideways and hang slightly.* M. × media *has 17-21 leaflets with many long, erect racemes of lemon-yellow flowers. It includes several cultivars, all of great beauty.*

Mahonia japonica
(mature leaf)

Mahonia japonica
(young leaf)

Mahonia japonica

Mahonia × media

leaflets, giving the plant a light, feathery appearance. Its many low inflorescences at the end of each branch carry hundreds of small, deep yellow flowers, the whole being held upright. It has been hybridized with M. *japonica* to give a group of plants that are collectively named M. × *media*; these are all good and are rather hardier than M. *lomariifolia*. Among M. × *media*, 'Charity' can become very tall and spindly with all its leaves at the top of the plant but it is greatly improved by being cut back hard one spring, after which it will take on a bushy, well-furnished habit. 'Winter Sun' and 'Buckland' are two very good, fairly fast-growing clones with fine heads of flowers.

Perhaps the most magnificent of all the mahonias is M. *acanthifolia*. It suffers from the stigma of suspect hardiness but it is a plant that is much hardier than commonly thought and, given a sheltered position, will grow to be a tree some 7.5m/25ft high. Its foliage is much divided and it flowers in early winter with long clusters of lemon-yellow blooms like small bells.

Wonderful plants as the more elegantly leafed mahonias are, none of them can surpass M. *japonica* for the contribution it makes to the winter garden. They all flower for part of the season, but M. *japonica* starts at the end of autumn and carries on right into the spring. In colder climates, substitute M. *bealei* or M. *aquifolium* for the less hardy M. *japonica*. Nevertheless, the whole of this superb genus will always provide a striking presence all the year round, which is enhanced after flowering by berries of purple or black overlaid with a rich bloom. I have seen Russell Lupins planted with telling effect in front of mahonias – an association that increases the effectiveness of both plants, with the stately herbaceous plant echoing the majesty of the shrub. However, mahonias generally demand to be one of the elements in a contrast.

Camellias associate particularly well with them. An outlying group of mahonias will make a marvelous foliage contrast with the rounded, polished evergreen leaves of camellias. Sasanqua varieties will provide a particularly strong contrast to the mahonias and the flowering seasons will coincide when M. *japonica* is present. Where the climate is only just warm enough for sasanqua camellias, the white variety, *Camellia sasanqua* 'Narumi-gata', may be relied upon to flower fairly reliably, whereas other sasanquas need sunny summers to induce their flower buds.

Scented flowers

Scent is a quality that many winter-blooming shrubs have in common, possibly because the business of attracting pollinators in winter is one in which demand outstrips supply. The shrubby loniceras (honeysuckles) demonstrate this feature to a large degree and their conspicuous, white or cream flowers are lovely to look at as an added bonus. *Lonicera fragrantissima* is a plant of the early spring but *L. standishii* flowers in the middle of winter, and when the two are hybridized they produce *L.* × *purpusii*, which is also

A winter comparison
The appeal of this little garden does not rely on flower color at all, but on the harmony of the rounded forms of the clipped evergreen shrubs and the leaves of the bergenias, and the contrasting geometric shapes of the steps and patio. The whole scene presented by this garden is rich, neat, green and pleasing throughout the year.

winter-flowering. *L. standishii* is otherwise very similar to the later-flowering species and shares with it the bonus of red berries in early summer; the hybrid is more vigorous than either of its parents and has larger, creamy, highly scented blooms. All these plants are relatively hardy. Put them close to the house or a path so that you can imbibe the scent without getting muddy and wet.

The daphnes are wonderful plants for winter and early spring fragrance. A good winter-flowering one is *Daphne bholua*. The species varies from evergreen or nearly so to completely deciduous, but the flowers are almost always purple-pink, twenty or so in terminal clusters, and very sweetly scented indeed. The succession of blooms goes on right through the winter months and is followed by black fruits on a plant some four feet high or more. *D.b.* 'Gurkha' is a fine form. *Daphne odora* suffers from lack of hardiness, but the variety 'Aureomarginata' is tougher. *D. odora* hybridized with the late-spring flowering *D. collina* is *D. × hybrida* and is even hardier and flowers early in winter. In still colder gardens use *D. × burkwoodii*.

Perfect for winter scent, especially for small gardens, are the curious little sarcococcas. *Sarcococca hookerana* is a small or dwarf shrub with an erect habit and neat glossy leaves. The flowers have one of the headiest perfumes of all garden plants. Some say that it is not very hardy but I have always found it to be so; it may be safer to grow the form *S.h.* var. *digyna* which is a more slender plant and is hardier according to some authorities. Sarcococcas tolerate shade very well and can be planted almost anywhere. They have a preference for limestone but succeed perfectly well in soil which is acid.

Viburnum tinus flowers throughout the winter and has glossy green leaves. However, in a genus noted for fragrance it is scentless. Much better is *V. farreri* (formerly *V. fragrans*). It is a deciduous shrub which, if given room, can spread to about nine feet and be as much high. It is rather huffily erect when it is young but becomes more

rounded as it gets older (as most of us do). The flowers are produced along the branches as well as at the ends and are rose-pink in the bud, opening to white. The scent is superb and does not become cloying as you come close to the flowers. *V.f.* 'Candidissimum' is a variety with white flowers with no trace of pink; its scent is just as good.

However, if I were to allow myself just one winter-scented viburnum, it would be *V. × bodnantense* 'Dawn'. Its flowers are larger – and appear on a bush which is even more good-looking – than *V. farreri* and are richly red in the bud, opening to white with a strong pink flush. The form *V. × b.* 'Deben' is lighter in color and whiter when open. This is such a good plant that a small group could occupy a place anywhere in the garden, but preferably near a path, as with all scented plants.

Viburnum × bodnantense 'Dawn'

Plants for height and depth

In a genus from which one expects scent, it is disappointing that its best winter-bloomer is almost scentless, but that should not stop you from growing *Jasminum nudiflorum*, the Winter Jasmine. It is not a climber but can be trained on a wall or even over a pergola as long as it is tied in. It is a beautiful plant which bears its fairly large yellow flowers right the way through the winter months. If you have something unattractive in your garden, such as an ugly wall or a none-too-pretty bank, this will cover it and make the spot a focus of winter attention. As its name suggests, it flowers when the branches are leafless but when the foliage does appear it is attractive, though subdued.

Jasminum nudiflorum

An evergreen clematis that will do similar jobs is *Clematis cirrhosa*, which flowers all winter. The fairly large blooms, about 6.5cm/2½in across, are of a very light yellow that is almost white. The variety *C.c. balearica* is more robust and its divided leaves take on bronze or purple hues in winter which emphasize the creamy yellow of the flowers and accentuate the maroon spots inside them.

Acacia dealbata

Winter flowers
A selection of attractive winter-flowering plants can be seen above.

The lovely *Acacia dealbata*, with its ferny, gray-green foliage, is extremely fast-growing and can approach a height of 9m/30ft in only eight years from seed. Because of this, it is a tree that, if lost through frost (usually borne on a chilling wind), can quickly be replaced. It is one of the great joys of the year when, in late winter, it becomes wreathed in myriads of tiny yellow pompoms on upright inflorescences. There is, too, the scent, which is more noticeable on warm days and even more so when the flowers are cut and taken indoors. It will grow wherever frosts are of short duration and where there is shelter from wind; in such conditions it will take a lot of cold without damage to the evergreen foliage or to the buds (although a long, cold winter may make it flower much later). Of all the winter-flowering plants it is the most springlike and it flowers right at the end of winter. What is more, it is a tree of great beauty at all times of the year.

Berries and fruit

Berries and other fruits brighten up the winter garden wonderfully, if the birds have not eaten them in autumn. When birds are faced with a long and varied menu, their depredations will not be so noticeable, but in a bad year there will not be much to see in winter unless the gardener has chosen plants that can be relied on to keep their fruits well into that season.

Shrubs

Pyracanthas are preeminent among plants with longlasting fruits. Their stiff habit makes them ideal wall shrubs and they are among the most easily grown of all shrubs, tolerating any soil; in fact the poorer the soil and the more restricted their roots, the more they will flower and fruit. When well suited they will become a frothing mass of white flowers in summer and will be entirely covered with berries throughout the late autumn and the winter. The fruits are yellow, vivid orange or bright red and the three colors

LEFT *The glossy leaves of* Skimmia japonica *have a freshness that lasts all the year round. They provide the perfect background for the plant's shiny, bright red berries, which are extremely long-lasting.*

BELOW *The bright yellow berries of* Ilex aquifolium *'Bacciflava' make an interesting change from the more traditional red of other species. The tree can be relied on to bear heavy crops of berries in most years.*

115

combine well when grown alongside each other. Pyracanthas are often recommended for north- or east-facing walls. In such conditions they will certainly bear berries and they are useful plants for that reason alone. However, in milder climates their greatest glories are seen when grown facing south. In full sun and in a sparse soil they make a wonderful spectacle, especially in the winter sun. They are all evergreen, and can also be grown as freestanding shrubs, although the sheer wealth of berries cannot be as good as when they are on a sunny wall.

Cotoneasters are berrying shrubs that vary from very large plants to minute, thymelike carpeters. The evergreen species are the best for pleasing shape and habit, abundant flowers, late berrying and attractive foliage.

Cotoneaster hybridus pendulus is a glossy-leaved evergreen which has arching, pendulous branches that give the plant the appearance of a weeping tree, if it has been trained up on a stem – the best and most effective way of growing it, as it will then take its place as a specimen in its own right, either among shrubs or as a member of a group of small trees growing in grass. Its berries are bright red and last for most of the winter. The Watereri Group of *Cotoneaster* contains some good all-seasons plants. You can use their tall, arching branches with their pointed, evergreen foliage and bright red or yellow berries at the boundary of a garden where a tall but informal screen is needed.

Selecting two cotoneasters for the small-to-medium-sized garden is fairly easy. *C. glucophyllus* var. *vestitus* is a good-looking species all of the year, flowers profusely in midsummer, and only shows color in its berries as the worst of winter sets in. *C. harrovianus* does the same and its flowers are rather more showy. What is certain with these two plants is that the birds will have no interest whatever in their berries until well into winter.

Among smaller evergreen shrubs, *Skimmia* is a genus that requires the presence of a male plant for berries to appear on female ones. Most of

the female forms bear red berries of a particularly bright and eye-catching red. *S. japonica* has fragrant flowers in early spring, is easy to grow on any soil and its berries last the whole season through. It looks best with other shrubs of similar structure. *S.j.* 'Foremanii' is about the best clone for vigor and number of fruits. The species *S. reevesiana* is a lime-hater but on the other hand is a hermaphrodite and has dark red berries which last so long that they can be overtaken by the flowers. The best male skimmia is *S.j.* 'Rubella', which does not have berries in winter, but plays its part in the winter garden by displaying tight bunches of maroon-red buds throughout the season, before they open in spring to reveal white flowers.

Trees

Holly berries can be bright red, like those used for Christmas decoration, dark red or yellow. What you choose will be a matter of taste but the tree itself should have something about it that appeals to you besides the berries, since hollies can be boring and their uncompromis-

ABOVE *The colorful red of this heavy crop of cotoneaster berries is made even brighter by the whiteness of the snow and the plant's evergreen leaves. The berries will last well into the winter.*

RIGHT *Ilex crenata 'Latifolia' is a slow-growing holly, making a medium-sized shrub. Although its leaves are plain, deep green, the effect of frost is to make them appear to be beautifully and evenly variegated.*

ingly rigid habits are hard to place in the garden, especially as they draw attention to themselves in winter. A good plant is *Ilex × altaclarensis* 'Camelliifolia' which has large, shiny spineless evergreen leaves like those of a camellia, purple stems and large red berries. Its habit is more relaxed than many hollies and it is a very beautiful, medium-sized pyramidal tree. *Ilex aquifolium* 'Ovata Aurea' is marginally variegated with gold and is another good plant whose leaves contrast well with its purple shoots; it is a male tree and, so, useful for fertilization.

Among other species of hollies, *I. insignis* is outstanding because of its enormous leaves. At first they are smaller and spiny and then, as the plant matures, they can be as much as 20cm/8in long and are almost spineless. The berries are large too, and red. *Ilex dipyrena* is a most elegant small tree with a smooth, gray-tan trunk, long, lightly spined, willowlike leaves, and dark red berries. It is perfectly capable of seeding itself when it is enjoying life. Where winters are severe, use *Ilex opaca* in place of these other more tender evergreen species.

Members of *Sorbus* that have yellow or white berries, particularly the latter, tend to keep their fruits for a very long time, while their red-berried cousins lose theirs before winter starts (although the longest-lasting berries of all are pink and belong to *Sorbus insignis*; they last until the middle of spring). *S. hupehensis* is a tree of strong growth which can attain 15m/50ft but which is usually seen at not much more than 6m/20ft. Its leaves have 11 to 17 leaflets (one at the tip) and they have a very pleasant blue tinge. The berries are fairly large, white and held on long, bright red stalks. It should be planted where it can be readily seen and makes a good lawn specimen. *S. cashmiriana* is perhaps the gem of them all with even more leaflets and bunches of white marbles hanging on for a long time after leaf-fall. The autumn color of both species depends on the soil in which it is grown and varies from yellow to a mixture of yellow and red.

Crab apples have two main seasons of value, but only a few keep their fruits on the tree well into or right through the winter. Those with bright red fruits, like those of *Malus* 'Red Jade', whose blossoms are white and pink, and 'Red Sentinel', which has white flowers in spring, show up best. 'Crittenden' is a compact tree with pink blossoms and very heavy crops of bright red fruits; 'Almey' has flowers that are unusually large and red and its fruits are almost orange. Of all the crabs the one which has the most presence is a small tree which has a pyramidal habit of growth, becoming more spreading as it gets older. This is *Malus* × *zumi* 'Calocarpa', a bearer of persistent fruits of a cheerful red.

There are two thorns that are of superb garden value. *Crataegus durobrivensis*, an American tree, has white flowers that, at 2.5cm/1in across, are the largest in the genus and its large, glistening, crimson fruits persist until midwinter. *C.* × *lavellei* is a French hybrid which has

An all-seasons garden should look inviting in winter, and a tall clipped hedge, as well as providing an attractive permanent feature, will protect from cold winds. There is so much to see and appreciate in this winter garden that it will be a pleasure to venture out and linger by the seats in the shelter of the enveloping green hedge.

flowers that are very nearly as large and are also white. It is one of the few thorns which has really attractive foliage and the orange-red berries, which are 2cm/¾in in diameter, are borne throughout the winter. A third thorn, *Crataegus stipulacea*, is unusual in that it is a Mexican tree that can be grown in the milder parts of Europe and some wintry places in the United States and it is almost thornless. Its berries are yellow, very large and very persistent.

Positioning

The positioning of plants with fruits and berries needs some care. White or light-yellow ones are often inconspicuous unless seen from a nearby path. The white-berried species of *Sorbus* occur on trees that are small, so it is a good idea to plant them near vantage points from which they can be appreciated at something like close quarters. Red and orange berries are highly conspicuous and show up well from afar, but they often do not last, as they are the ones the birds like best. When they are left alone it is, sometimes, because they are sited near areas of constant human activity. It follows that you should also plant bird-fancied berries as near to the house or any well-used path as is practicable, or close by the main thoroughfare that passes the house.

If you grow the old-fashioned and species roses (see p. 76) with other shrubs, their bright hips will give color among the shrubs in winter. They will be the more effective for being planted at or toward the fronts of shrub borders and at intervals between other plants of similar sizes. As with so many other color effects, a background of green will make the colors seem to be even more vivid.

This same green background is given to the red berries of evergreen trees and bushes, such as holly and skimmia, by their own leaves and, because the berries show up so well, these plants can be planted at a greater distance from your winter vantage-points than those deciduous plants that bear fruit.

The view from the house

Winter weather will prevent much gardening being done, but the garden can still be enjoyed during that season and, what is more, enjoyed in comfort. It is a sybaritic delight to be able to look out upon a scene of chilly beauty from an environment of warmth.

The winter garden should be designed for such enjoyment. Prune away all flower stems and untidy growth so that the intricate rosettes of sedums and the gray foliage of catmint will hug the ground in stillness. Dwarf or very small shrubs – the low mounds of *Ceanothus thyrsiflorus repens* or the flat herringbones of *Cotoneaster dammeri* – will lie below window level and allow the eye to take in the green of the lawn and the plants that stand beyond it. Here the colored stems of *Cornus* and *Salix* 'Britzensis' are at a distance so that their yellows and reds appear almost as a mist against their evergreen neighbors but are close enough to show their structure, while the reds of rose hips and the gold of the smaller conifers will echo such tints. In the distance, where the taller evergreens

Grasses are the most informal of plants and their attractions last throughout the winter. They are best sited out of the wind, where they can maintain a restful air. Formal evergreen hedges can shelter and protect them and also benefit from the contrast they afford.

sway in the wind next to their stiller deciduous companions, the sense of cold is comfortably far off and their shapes can be appreciated the more for their movement.

If you plant a drift of *Cyclamen orbiculatum* so that they weave in and out of small shrubs near a path, place one or two beneath the window. They will produce their small red flowers, like tiny propellers, one winter day and induce you to wrap up and go out to see the rest of them. When you do venture out into the garden there will always be a surprise, like the first snowdrop or the determination of *Iris reticulata* 'Cantab' to get its sky-blue flowers above the snow.

LEFT Iris reticulata *defies the snow to announce the coming year.*

BELOW *The bold shapes and elegant arrangements of the permanent plants and garden features such as fountains in a formal garden provide a strong structure all year round. Indeed, a very formal garden can often look particularly attractive in winter when the shapes are emphasized and given extra light and shade by snow.*

PLANTS & CULTIVATION

PLANTING & PRUNING

BEFORE PUTTING YOUR hand in your pocket at a nursery, spend a little time making sure that the specimen you buy is the best of its type available. Look carefully at the plant and check that it has no obviously diseased or damaged wood or foliage, that it is a good shape and that it has a well-developed and healthy root system. Sometimes, especially with container-grown plants, you will see a lot of root material growing out through the drainage holes at the base of the container. In general, it is better not to buy a plant in this condition, since you will have to cut away much of the protruding root in order to free the plant from the container. Plants grown in containers that are too small for them can also become root-bound – the roots grow in circles and end up throttling each other. Do not buy root-bound plants unless it is the only way of obtaining a rarity, in which case you must try carefully to tease the roots apart.

Planting shrubs and trees

The first step when planting a container-grown shrub or tree is to remove it from its pot. This may sound ridiculously elementary but is, in fact, often not as easy as it sounds, and many plants are damaged during the process. The polyethylene bag type of container can be removed by slitting it carefully with the tip of a sharp knife, from the bottom upward, and peeling the plastic away from the contents.

To remove a rigid pot, turn the plant upside down (or as near upside down as possible) with your fingers splayed out over the surface of the soil and then strike the rim of the pot with a light upward blow with your free hand. If this doesn't work or if the plant is too big, strike the rim a sharply downward blow on to any convenient solid object, such as the top of a low wall.

Soil preparation

Merely making a planting hole a little bigger than the diameter of the pot and then filling in the gap around the root ball with soil is bad practice. First, you must dig over an area of soil at least 90cm/36in in diameter and to a depth of at least 30cm/12in, clear out any weeds, and incorporate manure or leaf-mold. Then make the planting hole, insert the root ball into place, fill in the gap with soil and firm the soil with your foot. By preparing the area surrounding the planting hole in this way, the plant will be able to spread its roots into friable, fertile soil, and you will also be sure that there are no roots of perennial weeds nearby.

Bare-rooted trees

To prevent trees (and large shrubs) becoming root bound, many nurseries grow larger specimens in the open ground, instead of in containers. Trees grown this way will be bought bare-rooted (with no soil ball surrounding the roots). Soil preparation is, however, the same as

Planting a tree
Prepare the planting site as described in the text, and check the depth of the hole using a straight piece of wood to ensure that the soil level will correspond exactly to the old nursery mark. Before planting the tree in its hole, hammer two hardwood stakes treated with a nontoxic preservative securely into position, joined at the top by a cross-piece, as shown above. Next, spread the roots of the tree out in the hole, trickle soil between them and fill up the rest of the hole, firming as you go. Using a proper tree tie, secure the trunk of the tree to the cross-piece, so that the lower part of the tree will be held steady in windy conditions while still allowing the top of the tree to move.

122

Planting clematis

We have already seen that clematis are among the most useful plants for extending all-seasons gardening into the vertical plane. These lovely plants are so often lost through bad planting that it is worth making sure that you do the job properly, right from the outset.

Whatever support is going to be used, the principles of planting remain the same. Dig a large hole, twice the depth of the container that the clematis comes supplied in and at least 60cm/14in across. Break up the bottom of the hole and add well-rotted manure (as you would for any plant) but, with clematis, place the plant more deeply in the hole than is usual so that the new soil level will be at least 5cm/2in higher up the stem than the level in the container. This will encourage stem buds to grow from below soil level if the stem should be damaged in any way. 'Plant' a strong bamboo cane at the same time and attach the stems of the clematis to it using proper plant ties.

Wherever a clematis is planted, but particularly at the base of a wall or under trees where the soil is often dry, you must pay great attention to watering in the first couple of years. In dry weather in the year after planting, water should be given in gallons rather than in pints. It is a good idea to plant the clematis away from the wall or tree, and to angle the cane, with the stems attached, toward it. You may have to attach some light plastic netting to a tree trunk to provide initial support. Finally, place some flat stones over the soil covering the roots of clematis, since these are plants that enjoy sun on their leaves and flowers but a shaded, moist root-run.

Anti-mouse guard
Mice love to gnaw the stems of clematis, so it is a good idea to make a guard for the lower part of the plant. Surround the bottom 15cm/6in of the plant with fine-mesh chicken wire and ensure that the lowest 5cm/2in of the wire is below soil level.

---

for container-grown plants, although the area of dug soil may well need to be larger, since the planting hole itself must be large enough for the roots to be spread out fully and without their ends turning up at the edge of the hole. With the tree in place, now is the time to drive a stake into the bottom of the hole. Fine, friable soil and well-rotted manure is then trickled through the roots and the tree given a light shake occasionally in order to settle the soil closely around the roots.

By using a flat piece of wood laid across the hole as a gauge, you can ensure that you plant the tree at exactly the same depth as it was in the nursery – you will be able to see the 'nursery mark' as a dark line round the stem (see opposite). Once you have covered the roots, stamp firmly on the soil to remove any air pockets and to stabilize the tree and so prevent slight movements of the stem disturbing the roots. You can now fill up the rest of the hole and lightly firm the soil. As with any plant, the next stage is to water-in, using a lot of water, thus establishing even closer contact between soil and roots.

Staking

The whole practice of staking has been subject to some radical rethinking recently. It has been noticed that trees that have been staked do not always stand up to winds as well as they should, after their stakes have been removed, while those that have been allowed some freedom of movement in their upper parts do much better. Also, stakes have to be driven in about one-third of their length, and the removal of long stakes often causes root damage. If, when removing the stake, it should break, then the decaying wood can be a source of disease. The modern practice is to use stakes that support only the lower third of the tree, the rest being allowed to move with the wind (see opposite).

Proper tree ties are by far the best thing to use and they can be adjusted, as the tree grows, to accommodate its increasing girth. Nylon twine should never be used. It has no 'give' and can cause an indentation in the stem, at which point the tree is prone to snap if subjected to particularly strong winds.

Pruning

There is more nonsense talked about pruning than about almost anything else in gardening. For most of the plants used in the all-seasons garden, pruning can usually be confined to the removal of dead, unsightly or unwanted wood, which can be carried out at any time, and to 'renewal' pruning.

Renewal pruning

Renewal pruning is best carried out in late winter or early spring. It does not matter if a year's flowers are lost, since the plant can concentrate on putting on growth. *Cytisus battandieri* (the Pineapple Broom) is a good example of a plant that benefits from renewal pruning. Since its growth is fast, it can easily become lanky and top heavy, and it will soon lose its effectiveness as a flowering tree if left untended. Its branches are richly furnished with dormant buds and, if the plant is cut back hard, these will quickly burst into growth, making a new framework of flowering branches. Old camellias and rhododendrons also respond well to this treatment, and they can be cut back a long way into really old wood.

Hydrangeas should be renewal pruned every three years or so and some of their branches removed at ground level, especially those that are thin and spent-looking and unlikely to bear flowers. If you do this while deadheading the plants in early spring, strong, stout flowering shoots will grow and may flower in the same year. Dead heads should be removed every year back to the first pair of strong buds.

Wisterias, unless growing into a tree, where the flowers need to be higher, must have their growths cut back to within two buds of their origins in the second half of the summer. This will produce short flowering spurs instead of long shoots that make nothing but foliage. *Vitis* 'Brant' requires the same treatment if it is to bear fruit, but do the job in winter when the plant is dormant.

Pruning trees

To grow trees with clear boles (trunks), you will have to remove their branches progressively, from the bottom upward. Use a sharp pruning saw for this job, and do it while the branches are young. Otherwise, disease can enter the large cut left by an older branch and the tree may never succeed in closing the wound. It is best to prune tree branches a few at a time over a number of years, preferably in spring. Do not paint the pruning wounds, as this practice can in some cases actually harm the tree.

Pruning clematis

Clematis are normally pruned to ensure that the plants have flowers from their bases upward, so those that are to be grown into trees or through shrubs do not need to be pruned, since the only flowers that will be effective will be those at the tops of the plants. On pergolas and walls, on the other hand, you will want the flowers lower down on the plants and the plants will, therefore, need to be pruned in order to achieve this.

Clematis that flower in late spring and early summer do so on the wood produced in the previous year. With these types, the spent flowering growths should be removed immediately after flowering. Those that flower in late summer and autumn should be pruned hard (to within 30cm/12in of the ground) in early spring. The very early flowering clematis, such as C. *montana* and C. *alpina* need have only dead or weak stems removed after flowering.

Pruning old-fashioned roses

Strictly speaking, the different classes of old roses require slightly different pruning regimes. However, if you adopt the same technique for all of them, you will achieve the main aims of pruning, which are a succession of strong, new growths from the bases of the plants and the avoidance of damage through their being rocked by the wind, especially in winter. If old, thin or spindly growth is regularly removed, cutting as low down on the plant as you can, you will make

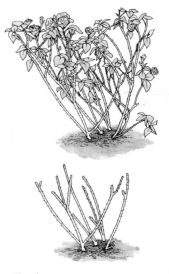

Shrub roses
To prune an old-fashioned shrub rose, remove crossing and inward-growing shoots and any weak, spindly growths. Reducing the strong, healthy growths by approximately one-third will encourage side growth and reduce the danger of wind-rock, which causes broken roots and weakened stems.

room for new growth to sprout from the burr at the base of the plant. If, after flowering, all long growths are reduced by a third (or by a half in windy gardens), the danger of wind-rock will be much reduced (see opposite).

Old roses are not meant to be pruned hard like modern ones; think of them as shrubs and treat them accordingly. Bourbon roses and Hybrid Perpetuals can be pruned harder than others to some advantage, but it should still be done after flowering has finished. At the end of winter, cut back any wood that has suffered frost damage to a good bud on sound wood.

Several sorts of these roses, in particular the repeat-flowering ones, can have their flower bearing increased dramatically. Instead of shortening the longest growths, bend them down so that you can anchor their tips to the ground by pegs or attach them to the bottom of an adjacent rose. By doing this, flower buds will be encouraged all along the arching branch and not just toward the end, thus making an enormous difference to the appearance of the bush when it flowers. Cut these growths away completely after flowering has finished when the new ones are tied down in their turn.

Plants on walls

Much has been written in this book about growing plants on walls. What confronts many gardeners, though, is the problem of training and supporting the plants, which is not as easy as many think.

Supporting

To support most plants, stretch wires horizontally along the wall at intervals of about 76cm/30in. Use wire of about 10 gauge, which should stand a few centimeters away from the wall surface on proper masonry fittings, obtainable from most large garden centers. It is essential that the anchorages at the ends should be perfectly firm and capable of taking the considerable weight of mature plants. You should also incorporate wire tensioners in each individual strand of wire.

Training

As the plant grows upward, tie its stem to each wire in succession. You can tie the branches in either horizontally or, more usually, at an angle of some 40° from the vertical (see right). *Clematis montana* has soft stems that can be trained horizontally, as does the Passion Flower, while *Ceanothus arboreus* is better trained in a fan. Trees, such as *Cytisus battandieri*, are better tied in to the wires in the natural positions their branches assume. Those branches that grow away from the wall at right-angles, or thereabouts, should be pruned off at almost any time of the year (see pp. 124-5), but preferably after flowering. This advice also applies to any unwanted, unbalanced or ugly growth.

The idea behind this type of training is to display the flowers and attractive foliage to their best advantage. You should always bear in mind that tied-in plants can be used as hosts for climbers that may, themselves, need to be tied in and controlled by pruning. *Ceanothus arboreus*, for example, when fan-trained, will lose nothing with a white clematis, such as 'Henryi', growing through it, but the old flowering growths of the clematis should be cut back and removed completely after it has flowered.

Fan training

This is one good method of training a wall shrub, such as a ceanothus. Prune away all unwanted growths and tie the remaining shoots on to canes or sticks. Anchor these to the wall with wires in a fan shape.

PROPAGATION

AS ANYBODY WHO HAS visited a local garden center or nursery will know, buying plants, especially well-developed specimens, can be an expensive business. However, most of the techniques used by commercial growers in propagating plants can be practiced by even a modestly equipped gardener, with more than a fair degree of success.

Division

Division is a method of propagating multi-crowned herbaceous plants. With large clumps you should use two forks, back to back, as levers to make the initial, major divisions; further splitting is then done by hand. Discard the old, central parts of the plants and use only the young, vigorous crowns.

With smaller herbaceous plants, such as primulas, hold the whole clump in a bucket of water and gently wash the soil away from the roots. The crowns will then separate easily. You can use this same technique for clumps of asiatic gentians.

Dividing primulas
Once the roots are exposed, gently tease the individual crowns apart, discarding the older, central part and keeping only the vigorous new crowns for replanting.

Seed

One favored and highly successful technique of raising plants from seed is to use a free-draining peat-based potting mix, which should be just damp but never wet. Place a light mulch of sphagnum moss over the seed flat to help prevent damping-off (wilting of seedlings caused by fungal attack).

Seeds should be sown in flats or small pots and, in general, should be covered to the same depth as the size of the seed. Some, such as Primula, Meconopsis and Eucalyptus seeds, must never be covered. Also, some seeds will need to be stratified before sowing by subjecting them to

Propagators
The base of the frame of the propagator should be covered with thermostatically controlled heating cables under a layer of sand, on which you can stand your seed flats or individual pots. As an alternative to buying a propagator you can make a simple frame yourself. The base of the frame can be adapted from any wooden box. Stretch clear plastic over the lid to allow light to enter but not drafts.

alternate chilling and warming. Mix these seeds with damp sand in a plastic bag and put them in the salad tray of your refrigerator for a few days, alternating this with bringing them into a warm room for four or five days. Catalogs will state if seeds need to be stratified. Fern spores are an exception in that they prefer to be sown on sterilized soil-based potting mix, which must be kept below 50°F/10°C.

After sowing, use a watering can with an extremely fine rose to water the seeds. You can also place pots of fine seeds in a bath of water so that the water level is just below that of the soil. Remove the pots when the surface of the soil starts to darken.

After watering, put the flats or pots in airtight glass frames. Ideally, the frames should have a bed of sand laid over thermostatically controlled soil-heating cables (which are available from most nurseries), set to 60°F/15°C (see opposite), and they should be placed inside a glasshouse for best results. You will also need a spare, unheated frame to hold germinated seeds. Alternatively, you can buy an inexpensive propagator that will do the job, on a smaller scale, just as well. Once the seeds have germinated, water them.

Most seedlings should be potted on (placed in larger, usually into 6cm/2½in diameter, pots) when they have grown their first pair of true leaves, although small seedlings will be easier to handle at a later stage.

Cuttings

Tree and shrub cuttings are best taken when the new growths are 'half ripe'. As a guide to this condition, it is when shoots are firming up well and will not snap when bent to an angle of about 25°. If they pass 30° without snapping, they are probably too soft and will rot before rooting. Camellias, with the exception of the white-flowered ones, have a red flush to their new growths; the right time to take them is just a few days after this has disappeared. The exception to this are the forms of the species *Camellia*

reticulata, which will not grow from cuttings at all and need to be grafted – a technique too specialized for most gardeners.

Take cuttings just above a node (leaf joint) using pruners or a sharp knife, and trim them back to just below the lowest node on each cutting. Remove the lowest leaves cleanly and flush with the stem (see right). Most half-ripe shrub cuttings are about 7.5 to 10cm/3 to 4in long and should be inserted into cutting mix for about one-quarter of their length. Use a potting mix consisting of half peat and half sharp sand and always choose sphagnum peat in preference to sedge peat, which is greasy and nonfibrous in content. You can propagate in the same frame you use for seeds. It is a good idea to give the cuttings a spray with tepid water from an atomizing spray once a day – twice in hot weather. The cutting should receive as much light as possible, but not direct sunlight.

Pot the cuttings on into ordinary potting mix once they have rooted. You can tell when this is by gently tugging them – if they resist, then they have rooted. Don't be tempted to dig them up to have a look, since this will almost certainly damage any roots that have grown.

Labeling

Whatever method of propagation you use, be disciplined about accurate labeling. It is easy to think that you will remember what everything is, but you are bound to forget at some time, especially since many seedlings and cuttings look extremely similar. The label should follow the batch of plants from seed or cutting flat to pots, and it really is best to give each pot its own label in case they become mixed up with other batches. Include the full botanical name of the plant, its date of sowing or when it was taken as a cutting and make a note of where your material came from – friend, nursery and so on. The all-seasons gardener may also find it useful to record the flowering season of the plant, and the color of the blooms.

Potting cuttings
After taking a cutting (1) and trimming it (2), insert it into the potting mix so that the mix level is just below the leaf-joint of the lowest leaf (3).

127

Moving Plants

AT SOME STAGE, YOU will almost certainly have to move some of your trees and shrubs, either because you have made a mistake or to put them into their final places in your design. Some plants resent being moved, while others don't mind at all, but they are all bound by a golden rule that states: water lost by the leaves must never exceed the amount of water gained by the roots.

This adage explains all sorts of puzzles – why, for example, evergreens die when the soil is frozen. It is not from the cold but from drought; the leaves are losing more water than the roots can take up. Once you understand this relationship, you will appreciate the need to reduce the foliage of a plant whose roots have been damaged, as they so often are when plants are moved.

Lifting plants

The object is to lift the plant with as much of its roots intact as possible, and, if roots are lost, a similar proportion of the top of the plant must be cut away. If, for example, you determine that approximately a third of the roots are damaged during this process, then you must reduce the amount of branches and foliage by at least a third. This may sound drastic but it is absolutely essential for the well-being of the plant.

Even if you think you have caused no damage to the roots, you will most certainly have done some. The important feeding roots are extremely delicate and difficult to see, and so as a precaution you should always reduce foliage a little – by, say, 10 per cent.

The best time for lifting most shrubs and trees is in the middle of autumn when the soil is still warm and root activity can carry on for a considerable time. Plants with fibrous root masses and a few, if any, long, woody roots,

such as rhododendrons, camellias, heaths and heathers, can be moved successfully at any time, provided their root systems are preserved intact. However, where winters are severe, broadleaf evergreens are best moved in .early spring. Hollies can be safely moved at the beginning of autumn or in early spring in damp weather.

Very large rhododendrons can be moved because of their solid, fibrous root system – it is just a matter of brute strength. In practice, it is as well to leave them alone once they have reached about 2.5m/8ft for large-leaved species, or 1.8m/6ft for the others.

Making a trench

With plants whose root systems can be lifted intact, dig a circular trench at the limits of the roots and gently lever the plant out of the ground with undercutting.

For all other plants, dig a circular trench far enough away from the trunk so that as little damage as possible is caused to the roots. The radius of the trench will often be determined by the proximity of other plants – you must avoid damaging their roots during the digging. Once the trench is complete, gently tease the roots out from the soil with a fork, trying not to bruise the delicate terminal ones, until the plant is free. You may need to cut some vertical roots, but keep this to a minimum. Cut back any broken roots to undamaged tissue and put the plant in its new position immediately. Use the procedure already described for planting bare-rooted trees (see p. 122).

Difficult plants

Magnolias detest being transplanted because they have delicate storage roots that are easily damaged. If such damage does occur, the plant is likely to stop growing and then go into

Preparing the plant
After freeing the roots of the shrub or tree, wrap cloth round the lowest part of the trunk as a precaution against damage from the carrying rope. This is tied so as to grip the trunk tightly, while leaving a free loop.

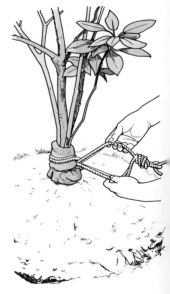

irreversible decline. If magnolias must be moved, do it in spring just before the blossoms appear. A certain amount of damage will be tolerated provided that the plant is able to repair itself quickly in the warm spring soil.

Although Dogwoods that are relatively small shrubs are not difficult to transplant, they sometimes react badly to being pruned. They must also be protected from accidental blows by a mower, which can kill these plants. *Stuartia*, which are related to the easily moved camellias, are best transplanted in the spring. They share with *Eucryphia* a fondness for having their roots shaded from hot sun, and it is a fair rule of thumb to take it that plants with this preference may not move well, since it is a sign that their roots are sensitive to damage.

Eucalyptus species are exceptional in several ways, not least in that moving them is a hopeless proposition. This is linked to their planting requirements. Unless they are planted in their final positions no later than three to four months after germination, they will never become wind-firm.

They must never be staked either – there is a saying in Australia that the bigger the stake used to support a eucalyptus, the bigger the tree when it falls down.

Carrying technique

If a plant is too heavy or unwieldy to carry easily, never try to move it alone, or you are likely to hurt both yourself and the plant. Always ensure that you have somebody to help you; carrying the plant on some tough burlap cloth should make the load easier to handle. Heavy plants may need three or even more people. One effective technique is to thread a stout pole through one loop of a rope that has been made in a figure eight; the other loop passes round the trunk of the plant. With one or two people on each end of the pole, trees and shrubs that would defy other methods can be moved (see below). This technique is particularly suitable for large rhododendrons, which will have a complete, and extremely heavy, root ball.

Lifting and moving the plant
Thread a pole through the free loop. With one or two people at either end of the pole, lift the plant free of the soil. Place the root ball on a large piece of burlap cloth, remove the pole, and carry the plant to its new situation in the sacking. At the new site, use the pole again to lift the plant into its hole.

BULBS-ON-BULBS

CONTRARY TO POPULAR belief, the depth at which bulbs are planted is not critical. The generally offered advice is that the bulb should occupy the lowest third of the hole into which it is planted – this is a good general guide, but you do not have to follow it slavishly. Indeed, anybody who has had to dig up bulbs that have been established for a number of years will have been astonished by the range of depths at which bulbs of the same species have settled.

The fact that bulbs move gradually up or down in the soil shows us a way of increasing the amount of flowers, and creating a succession of flowers, on one patch of ground – a particularly important consideration in small gardens.

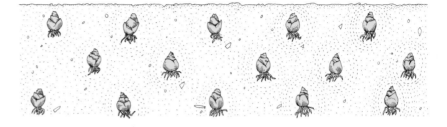

Layers of bulbs

Taking daffodils as an example of creating layers of bulbs, it is possible to plant bulbs at varying depths to produce dense patches of flowers extremely quickly. First, dig a hole about 23cm/9in deep (the size of the hole depends on the area of ground you have available), and place a layer of bulbs, about 7.5cm/3in apart, at the bottom. Cover these with just enough soil to hide them and then add two additional layers in the same way, so that the bulbs of each layer occupy the spaces between the bulbs below. Finally, add sufficient soil to bring the level up to that of the surrounding ground (see above).

Planting depths will vary according to the sizes of the bulbs. It is not a good idea to mix large daffodils with small, but those that flower at different times can be mixed to great effect.

Mixing bulbs

Where it is not necessary, in terms of tidiness, to remove the leaves of bulbs after flowering (which, in any case, should never be done until at least seven weeks from the fading of the last flowers, and eight is safer), you can mix genera. An ideal position for this would be an open area among shrubs. Here, smaller daffodils will give color before the shrubs flower, but for late summer and early autumn color you can plant galtonias in the bottom two layers of the hole alongside the daffodil bulbs.

Take care not to mix bulbs with different cultural needs. Those already mentioned need sun but do not require a period of dryness and heat in summer, and their position could well be shared by *Allium giganteum*, a tall plant with large heads of tiny lilac flowers in early to mid-summer. In mild gardens, the galtonias can share space with the evergreen watsonias. Hardier strains of these late-summer bulbs are gradually becoming available, and any losses owing to cold are quickly made up from the abundantly produced seed.

Since bulbs are usually inexpensive to buy, you should try experiments with mixing bulbs in your garden. Some very exciting results can be obtained, but there are two provisos. First, you can mix bulbs of different flowering periods but not of different needs and, second, you must feed the soil in early spring with a good general fertilizer, a mulch or both.

Planting bulbs
To increase the flowering capacity of any piece of ground, plant bulbs in three layers so that the bulbs below flower through the spaces left by those above. Because those lower down will flower later, this method extends the flowering period.

FEEDING

FOLLOWING CLOSELY AFTER questions concerning the correct way to prune plants (see pp. 124-5), gardeners' next most voiced worry is to do with how to feed their plants. This is because professionals, whose training has led them to think in terms of artificial feeds for everything that has its roots in the soil, have placed far too much emphasis on the subject. This attitude does little to help gardeners understand the needs of their plants.

Mulching and manuring

If plants are to grow well, the soil must have a high humus content and no amount of artificial additives will provide this element. Humus is an amorphous black gel formed by decomposing organic matter. It is not fibrous or open but it is derived from fibrous material, which, until it breaks down completely, is of an open structure and keeps the soil friable and well aerated. Part-decayed plant material is, therefore, essential, and the city gardener will have to make a special effort to come by it.

It is not essential, though, to travel hundreds of miles into the country in order to secure animal manure. Most large cities have breweries, and spent hops (after they have been stacked in the open for a year) make fine garden compost. The spent compost from mushroom growers is also very good, but never use it if you have an acid soil, since it contains lime.

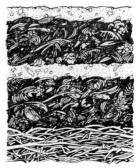

Making a compost pile
Garden compost is even better and it is easily made. All nonwoody material – except for pernicious weeds with creeping underground stems or persistent roots, such as docks, convolvulus or couch grass – should be made into a pile (see below), contained within an enclosure

Compost piles
Ideally, organic matter should be left to decompose for three years before it is ready for use. The easiest way of organizing this is to build three separate piles – one for each year. In very small gardens, however, where you have space for only one pile, use a design that allows you to take out decomposed material from the bottom of the pile, leaving the top material undisturbed. A layer of coarse material at the bottom, alternating layers of organic matter and soil and open-work lumber sides will allow air to circulate (see cut-away illustration above right).

of wood, wire or rigid plastic netting. Cover each 15-cm/6-in layer of vegetable material with 5cm/2in of soil. This will allow the bacteria present in the soil to get on with the job of breaking down the material into a usable form. If soil is at a premium, as will probably be the situation in a small garden, then you can use a brand-name compound to accelerate the decomposition process. Grass clippings are valuable once they have been well composted. Care needs to be taken, however, since, if used too soon, they remove nitrogen from the soil and become very hot; they may also contain seeds from lawn weeds, which will germinate and grow.

Ideally you should build three compost piles – one each year – and in year three start using the compost you laid down in year one, which by then should be a uniform mass of crumbly, soil-like material. These piles do not have to be large; they can be of a size to suit all but the tiniest of gardens.

Mulching

Mulching is simply a matter of spreading a layer of a suitable material – a mulch – over the surface of the soil. The depth of the layer will vary with the type of mulch used – but about 5cm/2in is usually right. Mulching serves several purposes: it greatly reduces the need for weeding and, to a large extent, the need for watering. It also prevents soil-splash on to small plants and garden labels, as well as feeding your plants.

You can use any of the manure or compost materials mentioned so far, or you can also use half-decayed leaves (nature's own mulch), peat and pulverized bark. The bark you buy in garden centers is stripped from trees used in the production of paper, and it is available in several grades, or degrees, of fineness; it really makes no difference which you buy. What is important, however, is that you use so-called 'composted' bark, which has been treated with a nitrogen compound. Without this additive, the bark will

Leaf mulch
Half-decayed leaves placed round the base of a plant make an excellent weed-suppressing, moisture-retaining mulch.

Feeding and protecting

Nature does not directly 'feed' plants in the wild, but she does provide nutrients that are often missing in the artificial environment of the garden. Bear in mind, though, that you are also trying to do a little better than nature and to produce plants that can be protected from some of the problems, diseases and pests that are found in nature.

Once plants are growing, it can be harmful, as well as unnecessary, to dig among them. Nature places the sources of plant food on the ground, and so should we. Once there, worms will take the material underground where it will rot down to make the minerals and salts that plants need, as well as the humus that conditions the soil.

Mulches of leaves, garden compost, composted bark and horse manure (well rotted, otherwise it contains too much ammonia, which is harmful) are all highly beneficial sources of plant food. Peat can be used, but it is important to realize that, of itself, peat has no food value. It is only when it has broken down and seems to have disappeared that it is doing any good; until then its use is only as a soil conditioner and an aerator.

Repeat-flowering roses, bred beyond the intention of nature to produce successive crops of large, complicated flowers, must be fed. Mulches are excellent for them, but it is a good idea to give the plants a periodic foliar feed as well. Because they are subject to insect attack and to fungal diseases, a two-weekly regime of spraying with a brand-name 'cocktail', containing an insecticide, a fungicide and a foliar feed, should start at leaf burst and carry on until the early autumn. Mulching before leaf burst will ensure that any fungal spores on the soil do not reach the new foliage through the medium of rain splashes from the soil.

There is no need to concern yourself with feeding beyond this in the all-seasons garden, and, similarly, there is little that the all-seasons gardener needs to worry about in terms of pests and diseases. Good cultivation will prevent most problems, while the ones that are bound to occur periodically, such as honey fungus, are beyond the control of the gardener anyway. Apart from these, there is little that is serious or should cause concern to the all-seasons gardener.

extract nitrogen from the soil as it breaks down, much to the detriment of the plants, which need nitrogen for growth. Alternatively, you can treat ordinary bark yourself with sulphate of ammonia, spread at about 30g per sq m/1oz per sq yd.

Mulching is an important method of introducing food to the roots of plants, such as magnolias and *Cornus* species, that must not be disturbed. Also, as your garden develops and the plants mature, you will find that it is almost impossible to fork material into the soil without causing damage, and so you will find yourself relying on mulching as a feeding method more and more.

Animal manure

Of all the animal manures, that from horses is the best, whether they have been bedded on straw, wood chippings, paper or peat. Like garden compost, manure should be kept until it is a uniform black mass. These days cattle manure is found only in the form of a slurry and is too liquid to be of any use; pig manure is offensively smelly; and manure from poultry is too strong in nitrogen.

Protection in severe winters

The all-seasons gardener can be an adventurous person, not averse to trying to grow plants that might be just a little tender. In most years this attitude will probably not result in any damage, but the occasional, severe winter may cause the death of some favorite plants.

It is just not worth growing plants that have to be protected every winter. For one thing, they will eventually become too large to be protected adequately and so can be regarded only as temporary inhabitants of your garden; however, those that need special attention only once every, say, 10 or 20 years, are worth every effort to include in your collection. For another, most forms of protection will look artificial and unattractive, and our all-seasons philosophy will not allow the winter garden to be marred in this way every year.

Methods of protection

The most basic form of protection for these sometimes-tender plants is to make sure that they are growing in a place that is out of the prevailing cold wind direction and that they are not growing in parts of the garden that are likely to become frost pockets. Evergreen trees offer the best protection of all, but if these are not already established you will have to provide some temporary wind protection for your smaller plants. Plants often die in winter from drought rather than simply from cold. Winds take moisture from evergreen leaves and frozen roots cannot replace it. A simple temporary screen (like the one shown here) will often save the life of a young plant which may well take severe weather unprotected when it is older.

Small plants that will, when older, stand up to fairly severe winters, can be protected when young with straw. Fluff some straw from a bale, lightly pack it round the plants and use string to hold it in place. The string need only be tight enough to compress the straw lightly (it should stay in place perfectly well even in the strongest wind), and air will still be able to circulate round the plant. Hay and wood wool will do the same job just as well.

It is a mistake to place plastic sacks over plants. They are just as likely to suffocate as you would be and, with the circulation of air cut off, they are very likely to rot. With a larger plant, you can tie straw lightly to its branches. This is a lot of work and it looks dreadful, but many a plant has gone on for a quarter of a century or more after such care, which was needed only for a week or two.

Wind protection
On the windward side of the plant, erect a frame covered with burlap or close-mesh plastic netting. The frame should have supports driven far into the ground and be guyed to pegs for extra strength.

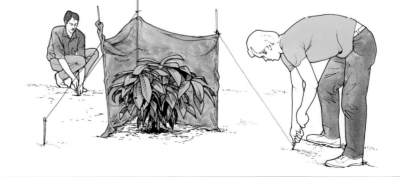

PLANT GUIDE

When using this plant guide, remember that two of the most important aspects of establishing a successful garden are the hardiness of the plants you use and the eventual size they will attain – and neither of these points is straightforward.

Hardiness

The concept of hardiness poses one of the most vexed problems in gardening, and the ability of a plant to survive depends on two factors – air temperature and wind speed. The effect of low temperature depends on its duration. Plants, for example, that will stand 14°F/−10°C and a 19-24 mph wind for 12 hours (or longer in still air) are here designated as having a hardiness rating of D or E. Plants that will survive still-air temperatures of 5°F/−15°C for long night periods but not all day for more than a day or two, and which will not tolerate such temperatures for more than about 12 hours in a 19-24 mph wind, are rated at C. Those in category B will tolerate temperatures as low as −4°F/−20°C with light wind for a few days and nights, while plants given rating A will take such temperatures with wind day and night for some days.

It must be emphasized that the table below should be taken as a general guide only. Local conditions will play their part, as will such things as topography and elevation. For example, some plants are less hardy inland than they are in coastal regions, even in the same conditions of temperature and wind strength.

Size

It can be very misleading to give the dimensions of plants in precise figures. The factors that govern the ultimate size of a tree or shrub are many and they often interact.

One of these factors is soil. In an impoverished soil a plant may well attain only half the height that it could reach in a well-nourished, deep loam. But it does not necessarily follow that a plant will be in poor health in a thin soil, and in some instances the smaller, more compact plant may withstand cold and wind better than its larger counterpart. Another influence is the elevation of your garden. The higher up your garden is the shorter the growing season will be and, therefore, the longer a plant will take to reach any given size. As elevation increases, the effect of wind is also more telling. Sea winds, as any coastal gardener knows, are stunting, and winds bearing frost will quickly reduce the height of most plants. The other major factors include latitude, the amount of shade to which a plant is subjected, the height of the water table in your garden and soil temperature.

Taking all these influences into account, the table below can be taken as a working guide only, but it gives you an idea of the sizes you could expect your shrubs or trees to attain in ideal growing conditions after a period of 20 years.

In the following guide, where information about a plant's flowers has been omitted, it is because they are insignificant.

HARDINESS

Hardiness Code	Lowest temperature tolerated	Duration	Wind strength
A	−4°F/−20°C and beyond	7 days and nights 14 days and nights	19-24mph Still air
B	−4°F/−20°C	7 days and nights 14 days and nights	4-12mph Still air
C	5°F/−15°C	Short periods of a few hours 7 days and nights with intervals of higher temperatures	19-24mph Still air
D	14°F/−10°C	12 hours 3 days and nights	19-24mph Still air
E	23°F/−5°C	12 hours 2 days and nights	19-24mph Still air to 12mph

NB: *Evergreens are more vulnerable than deciduous subjects. Frosts are more and more dangerous as spring progresses and plants come into growth.*

SIZE

Trees	
Small	Up to about 6m/20ft.
Medium	From 6m/20ft to 15m/50ft.
Large	From 15m/50ft upward.

Shrubs	
Dwarf	Up to 90cm/36in after many years.
Small	Up to about 1.2m/4ft.
Medium	From 1.2m/4ft to about 2.4m/8ft.
Large	From 2.4m/8ft upward.

TREES

*=evergreen	Flowers: season/color	Soil, situation and size	Out-of-flower qualities
*Acacia dealbata (E)	Early spring. Yellow.	Not on limestone. Medium.	Ferny, filigreed, gray-green foliage and green trunk.
Acer capillipes (A)	Spring. Green.	Any soil and situation. Small.	Striated 'snake' bark. Young growths and leaf-stalks are red. Good autumn color.
A. cappadocicum (A)	Spring. Yellow.	Any. Medium.	Broad, glossy, lobed leaves. Golden autumn color.
A.c. 'Rubrum' (A)	Spring. Yellow.	Any. Medium.	Young growths are blood red.
A. circinatum (A)	Midspring. Wine and white.	Any. Medium.	Round leaves are tinted in summer. Brilliant red and orange autumn color. A shrub unless trained.
A. davidii (A)	Spring. Yellow flowers, not very significant.	Any. Small.	'Snake' bark, striated green and white. Fruits are tinted red in autumn. Autumn foliage color is rich red and gold.
A. ginnala (A)	Late spring. Cream, very fragrant.	Small.	Spreading habit and attractive foliage. Autumn color is bright orange and crimson.
A. griseum (A)	Insignificant.	Any. Sun or part shade. Small.	Leaves turn a lovely mixture of reds in autumn. Mahogany, peeling bark shows orange new bark below.
A. grosseri (A)	Spring. Dull.	Any. Small.	'Snake' bark. Autumn color is brilliant red.
A.g. var. hersii (A)	As above.	As above.	Similar to the type but even hardier.
A. macrophyllum (A) (Alaskan forms are hardiest. Ranges to California.)	Midspring. Yellow flowers, scented.	Not on limestone. Large.	Largest leaves among maples. Autumn color is bright orange. Fruit has very large, bristly wings.
A. maximowiczii (A+)	Spring. Red.	Any. Small.	Striated bark. Leaves are red through the growing season; red-orange in autumn.
A. negundo var. violaceum (A)	Spring. Male and female on separate trees. Red.	Any soil but likes moisture. Medium.	Young shoots are purple, covered with white bloom.
A. palmatum 'Heptalobum Osakasuki' (A)		Moist soil and shelter from wind. Small.	Fresh green foliage. The blazing red of the autumn foliage is among the best of all trees.
A. pensylvanicum (A+)	Late spring. Yellow.	Cool, moist but well-drained site. Small.	Classical 'snake'-bark maple. Bark is striated white on pale green. Autumn color is bright gold.
*Arbutus × andrachnoides (E)	Autumn or spring. White.	Any. Shelter from wind.	Remarkable cinnamon-red trunk and branches. Dark green foliage and red 'strawberries' in autumn.

TREES

* = evergreen	Flowers: season/color	Soil, situation and size	Out-of-flower qualities
*Arbutus unedo (E)	Autumn. White.	Any (lime-tolerant member of Ericaeae). Small (medium in mild climates).	White flowers appear at the same time as the fruits in autumn. Fruits are similar to strawberries. Dark green foliage and attractive, deep brown bark.
Betula albo-sinensis var. septentrionalis (A)	Spring. Catkins.	Any. Small.	Beautiful, smooth, peeling bark, orange-tan in color with a pink-gray bloom. Light yellow autumn color.
B. jacquemontii (A)	As above.	Any. Medium.	Smooth, peeling bark, dazzlingly white.
B. lenta (A)	As above.	Any. Large.	Bark red-purple, young bark aromatic. Yellow autumn color.
B. papyrifera (A)	As above.	Any. Medium.	Brilliant white trunk even when very old.
Carpinus betulus 'Fastigiata' (A)	As above.	Any. Open position. Medium.	Lovely, light gold, late autumn color. Hoplike fruits after warm springs. Form is narrowly pyramidal when young, becoming broader later.
Cercis canadensis (B)	Early spring. Purple-pink on the branches or even on the trunk.	Sun lover. Good drainage; otherwise all soils. Small or medium.	Large seed pods remain on the tree through the winter. Flowers before the leaves appear.
*Cordyline australis (E)	White panicles in early summer. Scented.	Any. Sunny position. Small.	Not really a tree, but the "Cabbage Palm" is related to agaves. Tropical-looking with long, pointed evergreen leaves.
Cornus florida (A)	Each flower head is surrounded by four large white bracts. Midspring.	Acidic soil, particularly when rich, moist and well-drained. Sun. Large.	Rich red autumn color and showy red fruit. Branches end in unusually shaped shoots of a pink-purple tone.
C.f. 'Cherokee Chief' (A)	Large bracts, deep rose-red.	As above.	Red or red-gold autumn color.
C.f. 'Cherokee Princess' (A)	White, extra-large bracts.	As above.	Good autumn color in colder areas.
Cornus kousa (A)	Showy cream-white bracts. Late spring/early summer.	Moist, rich acidic soil. Sun or partial shade. Small.	Orange-red leaves and red fruits in autumn. Exfoliating bark in winter. Beautiful horizontal branching pattern.
C. nuttallii (C)	Large white bracts in late spring.	Not on limestone. Needs all available sun. Tends to die at maturity. Small/medium.	Golden foliage in autumn.
C. 'Eddies White Wonder' (B)	Bracts, much larger than above.	As above, but does not die early.	Better than C. nuttallii.
C. 'Ormonde' (B)	As above, and bracts take on pink tints.	As above.	Fine autumn color. Weeping form greatly enhances flowering effect and gives all-year-round impact. Very rare but becoming available.
Crataegus crus-galli (A)	White. Early summer.	Any. Sunny position. Small.	Leaves turn brilliant scarlet in autumn. Deep red, 13mm/½in fruits persist until the following spring.

* = evergreen	Flowers: season/color	Soil, situation and size	Out-of-flower qualities
Crataegus × lavallei (A)	White. Large. Early summer.	Any. Sunny position. Small/medium.	Distinctive long, glossy leaves remain until winter. Orange-red fruits last all through winter.
C. monogyna 'Biflora' (A)	White, scented. Late spring/early summer.	Any. Sunny position. Small.	Apart from main flowering season, it also flowers during mild spells in winter.
C. viridis (A)	White. Late spring.	Sun. Medium.	Silver bark. Prolific orange-red fruits.
Embothrium coccineum 'Lanceolatum' (E)	Scarlet. Late spring/early summer.	Lime-free soil. Sun or part shade. Small.	Only partly evergreen but other forms are hardiness C and are less floriferous. Its color at the time of year is too good to omit.
Eucalyptus coccifera (E)	White. Summer.	Any good soil, except limestone. Sun, shelter from wind. Medium.	Ash-gray, sickle-shaped evergreen leaves, peppermint scented. Flaking bark. It withstands severe frost. Pretty seed capsules persist.
E. gunnii (E)	White. Summer.	As above. Large.	Blue leaves, round or sickle-shaped. Trunk is blue/white/gray. It is the hardiest of the eucalypts and it can be stooled to produce a multi-stemmed, round-leaved bush.
E. niphophila (E)	White. Summer.	As above. Medium.	Broadly sickle-shaped, gray leaves with orange petioles. Bark becomes a patchwork of gray, green and cream.
E. parvifolia (E)	White. Intermittent.	Will tolerate limestone. Sun and shelter from wind. Medium.	Narrow, blue-green leaves. Buds and seed capsules are attractive.
E. pauciflora (E)	White. Spring/summer.	Any good soil. Sun and shelter from wind. Small.	Trunk and branches are white. Long, blue-gray sickle-shaped leaves.
Fagus sylvatica 'Pendula' (A)		Any good soil. Large.	The most spectacular weeping tree. Highly architectural winter effect.
Fraxinus excelsior 'Pendula' (A)		Medium.	Similar to the above tree but on a considerably smaller scale.
Gleditsia triacanthos 'Sunburst' (A)		Any good soil. Plant against a green background. Medium.	Golden foliage becoming a little green toward the end of the season.
Griselinia littoralis (E)		Any good soil. Withstands coastal conditions in mild areas. Medium/large.	Broad, apple-green leaves all the year round. 'Variegata' is boldly marked with cream but hardiness is E only.
Hoheria sexstylosa (E)	White. Late summer/early autumn.	Sunny spot on a good soil. Medium.	Very attractive foliage all the year round in mild areas. Overall 'feathery' appearance.
Ilex	There is a very large range of hollies. Some are trees while others are shrubs. Berrying species and varieties should be chosen for all-year effect but other characteristics will largely be a matter of the style of the garden and the preference of the gardener. Like anything else, they should not be overdone, but they will play an important part in winter gardens in cold areas.		
Laurelia serrata (E)		Any. Sun or part shade. Small/medium.	Evergreen, serrated, aromatic leaves of bright, light green.

TREES

*=evergreen	Flowers: season/color	Soil, situation and site	Out-of-flower qualities
Laurus nobilis (E)	Yellow. Spring.	Sun and shelter from wind. Small/medium.	Evergreen foliage with a strong aroma. As a free-growing tree, it has black-purple berries in early winter.
L.n. 'Aurea' (E)	Seldom flowers.	As above.	Not free-flowering or berrying but the tree becomes progressively more gold as it ages.
Liquidambar styraciflua (C)		Acidic. Large.	Maplelike foliage is attractive all season, and it becomes gorgeously crimson in autumn. Silver bark.
L.s. 'Lane Roberts' (C)		As above.	The best and most reliable clone for autumn color. Deep, black-crimson.
Liriodendron tulipifera (C)	Yellow-green 'tulips' with orange markings in mid-summer.	Any good soil. Large.	Leaves have a unique truncated shape. Butter-gold autumn color.
Magnolia campbellii (B)	Very large, pink flowers before leaves (at 20-30 years old). Early spring.	Lime hater. Flowers lost to frost in most years except in very mild areas.	Magnificent foliage. Seed pods open to show bright orange seeds.
M.c. var. *mollicomata* (B)	Even larger, purple-pink flowers appearing before the leaves (at about 12 years old). Flowers later in spring.	Lime hater. Hardier than the type, but needs protection from wind. Medium.	More reliable in flowering than the type. Foliage is just as good and seeds are orange-red.
M. delavayi (E)	Large, yellow and fragrant. Off and on all summer.	Tolerates limestone, but it must receive wind protection. Medium.	Very large, sea-green foliage, similar to that of a large-leaved rhododendron.
M. grandiflora 'Edith Bogue' (A)	Large, cream and fragrant. Late summer/early autumn.	Tolerates limestone with a good depth of soil. Medium, but it is best trained on a wall.	Very glossy, large green leaves. Hardiest of the *M. grandiflora* cultivars for northern USA.
M. × *soulangiana* (A)	There are many varieties of this hybrid. While they are very beautiful when in flower and their foliage is imposing, they do not offer much when out of leaf. They are irresistible for gardeners on lime-free soils but they grow to be large trees. The whites are better than other colors, which can be muddy, and care should be taken since not all varieties flower before the leaves.		
Malus 'Donald Wyman'	Large, white. Mid/late spring.	All soils. Sunny position. Medium.	Red fruits persist into winter. Disease-resistant.
M. 'Floribunda' (A)	Pale pink, fades white. Late spring.	As above except small.	Large crops of small, yellow fruits.
M. 'Red Jade' (A)	White and pink. Late spring.	As above.	Weeping habit. Small red persistent fruits.
M. 'Red Sentinel' (A)	White. Midspring.	As above.	Large crops of red fruits which persist all winter.
M. 'Wintergold' (A)	White, pink in the bud. Mid-spring.	As above.	Yellow fruits on long stalks persist until mid-winter.
M. × *zumi* 'Calocarpa' (A)	White, pink in the bud. Late spring.	As above.	Bright red fruits like large cherries persist all winter.

*=evergreen	Flowers: season/color	Soil, situation and site	Out-of-flower qualities
*Nothofagus fusca (E)		Any good soil. Shelter of other trees. Large.	Neat, small foliage with ruby-red tints that become pronounced late in the year. Straight-boled tree.
Nyssa sylvatica (B)		Acidic soils. Medium but wide spreading.	Handsome foliage turning brilliant red, yellow and orange in autumn.
Oxydendrum arboreum (A)	Clusters of white 'Lily of the Valley' flowers in summer.	Moist, acidic, organic soil. Full sun. Medium.	Outstanding red autumn color.
Paulownia tomentosa (A; flowers C)	Large, blue-purple foxgloves in midspring.	Deep soils. Sunny position and wind shelter. Medium.	Very large, heart-shaped, velvety leaves. Can be stooled to produce 2.5m/8ft shoots with leaves 60cm/24in across for a 'tropical' effect (but no flowers).
Prunus cerasifera 'Pissardii' (A)	Early spring. White, pink in the bud.	Any. Medium.	Flowers appear before the leaves. Foliage is dark red at first, becoming purple.
P. sargentii (A)	Single, pink. Early spring.	As above.	Dark chestnut bark. Foliage color turns very early to red and orange.
P. serrula (A)	Small, white. Midspring.	As above.	Smooth, mahogany bark that repays being polished with the hand. One of the best trees for ornamental bark.
P. subhirtella 'Autumnalis' (A)	Semidouble, white. Flowers lightly in autumn and again in spring.	Any. Small.	The main attraction of this tree is its autumn flowering.
Ptelea trifoliata (A)	Small, yellow. Early summer. The most scented flowers of any tree.	All good soils. Open position. Medium.	Autumn color is sometimes good. The variety 'Aurea' has light gold leaves that look well with Prunus cerasifera 'Pissardii'.
Pyrus salicifolia 'Pendula' (A)	Cream. Summer.	Any good soil. Open position. Small.	Small brown fruits. Light gray-green, willowlike foliage. Its weeping habit is attractive in winter.
Quercus	There are many species of oak, of which the two Quercus below are but a suggestion. There is a great diversity of size and shape in the genus, from very large trees to small shrubs. Just about all of them are good garden plants.		
Q. coccinea (A)		Acidic soil. Deep, loamy soil. Large.	Leaves turn brilliant scarlet in good years. Cultivar 'Splendens' is even better and more reliable. Perfect high canopy for rhododendrons.
*Q. ilex (E)		Deep loamy soil. Large, but stands clipping.	Perfect windbreak in milder areas. Its evergreen foliage is always a pleasant feature.
Robinia pseudoacacia 'Frisia' (A)	Unlike most forms, this seldom flowers. It is grown for its foliage.	Any good soil. Plant against green background. Small/medium.	Bright golden foliage from spring to leaf-fall, becoming richer as the season progresses.
Salix acutifolia 'Blue Streak' (A)	Catkins in spring before the leaves	Moist soil, sun or part shade. Not on limestone if dry. Small.	The species has long, pointed leaves and plum-colored, bloomy shoots. The shoots in the variety are dark purple.

TREES

*=evergreen	Flowers: season/color	Soil, situation and size	Out-of-flower qualities
Salix alba 'Britzensis' syn. 'Chermesina' (A)	Catkins in spring before the leaves.	Moist soil, sun or part shade. Not on lime if dry. Medium.	Long, silvery leaves. Branches brilliant orange-red.
S. daphnoides (A)	As above.	As above. Small but fast growing.	Long violet-colored shoots bearing a white bloom.
S. matsudana 'Tortuosa' (A)	Catkins before leaves, but not often borne.	As above. Small.	Branches ascrnding, twisted and contorted. An unusual and interesting winter waterside feature.
S. sachalinensis 'Sekka' (A)	Catkins in spring before the leaves.	As above.	Long, lanceolate foliage, silvery when undersides show in wind. Chestnut shoots that are oddly flattened and bent.
S. triandra (A)	Catkins with the leaves in spring. Fragrant.	As above.	Flaking bark.
Sorbus alnifolia (A)	White in dense bunches. Late spring.	Any well-drained soil. Medium.	Simple leaves turning bright orange in autumn. Dense foliage, but delicate branch tracery in winter. Red fruits early autumn, usually taken by birds. Best *Sorbus* for eastern USA.
S. aucuparia (A)	White. Late spring.	Coolness and moisture. Insect and disease prone in hot, dry situations. Small.	Red berries in autumn soon eaten by birds. Autumn color is good in cool, damp climates with short summers. Other species are better.
S. cashmiriana (A)	White flower, pink in the bud and pink-flushed.	Any good soil. Small.	Flowers unusually large for the genus. Large, white fruits not attractive to birds and persist. No autumn color as leaves fall very early.
S. commixta (A)	White. Late spring.	As above.	Excellent autumn color. Fruits in autumn bright red but eaten by birds. Feathery leaves.
S. 'Embley' (A)	As above.	As above.	Good, prolonged autumn color, always bright red. Orange-red berries bird-prone.
S. hupehensis (A)	As above.	As above.	Distinct blue tone to foliage, which turns red or orange according to soil. Fruits are large, white and pink-tinged borne on long, red stalks and are very persistent.
S. insignis (A)	White in large heads. Late spring.	Any good soil but give some wind protection. Small.	Large pinnate leaves that give a tropical effect. Heads of small pink fruits, many to a head, borne from autumn to spring.
S. 'Joseph Rock' (A)	White. Late spring.	Any good soil. Small.	Pinnate leaves, columnar habit. Autumn color is often a good mixture of gold and russet. Yellow berries, persistent.
Stewartia pseudocamellia (A)	White with golden-yellow stamens. Late spring/early summer.	Moist, well-drained, organic soil. Light shade. Medium.	Good companion for rhododendrons.
Styrax japonica (A)	White, snowdroplike flowers, hanging all along the lower sides of the branches.	Any good soil. Small.	Very neat foliage. Branches are nearly horizontal and look good in winter. Hanging, nutlike fruits in autumn.

CONIFERS

It is most important to obtain conifers from suppliers who are capable of giving accurate and genuine information about the ultimate dimensions, shapes and capacity for retention of foliage color of the plants. Otherwise grave disappointment can ensue long after any redress can be sought.

* = evergreen	Size and habit	Foliage color	All-seasons qualities
*Abies delavayi (A)	Medium. Conical.	Bright green above, silver below.	Cones 10cm/4in long, dark blue-violet in color.
*A. koreana (A)	Small/medium. Conical, neat.	Dark green above, silver below.	Cones are blue-purple and 7.5cm/3in long. Produced on very young trees.
*Chamaecyparis lawsoniana (A)	There are something like one hundred cultivars of this species, varying from dwarfs to large trees and including a great diversity of habit and foliage color. The species is a treasure-house for discerning gardeners, who should not be tempted to buy the first varieties they see.		
*C. obtusa and C. pisifera (A)	These two species will provide a very wide choice of smaller cultivars of all shapes and colors. Perhaps C.p. 'Boulevard' is one to be avoided, as its soft, blue foliage appears most attractive in nurseries but soon fades and browns off very easily.		
*Cryptomeria japonica (A cultivars)	The species is a large tree known as the Japanese Cedar. It has very good, rather ringleted, dense foliage and a soft, brown bark. The many cultivars are mostly slow-growing or dwarf.		
*Cupressus cashmiriana (E)	Medium. Conical, foliage soft and pendulous.	Dark gray-green.	A most beautiful, weeping tree, but tender.
Ginkgo biloba (A)	Large. Conical.	Green, turning gold in autumn.	Unique foliage, brilliantly gold before leaf fall. Strictly speaking, Ginkgo is not a conifer, but is often grouped with conifers.
*Junipers (A)	Of the enormous number of cultivars of species of juniper there are trees, shrubs and bushes of all sizes from large trees to prostrate mats (which make excellent ground cover). Colors vary and, as well as many shades of green, there are blue, silver, gold and green junipers.		
*Picea (A)	The species of spruce are almost all of great hardiness but often succumb to drought and heat, so they are best in colder areas. There are very large trees indeed and also a large number of slow-growing and dwarf cultivars. Most are green. P. orientalis is a large tree with speckled gray-fawn bark that curls into flecks on older trees – it is highly recommended for all-round effect.		
*Pinus (mostly A)	Pines are unsurpassed for dramatic form and for winter effect. Large trees are wonderful in very large gardens but smaller species, such as P. cembra and P. bungeana (the latter has beautiful bark) should be chosen. Dwarf forms, especially of P. sylvestris and P. mugo are of great architectural value in the context of small gardens or among small shrubs.		
*Thuja occidentalis, T. orientalis, T. plicata (A)	Thuja is a most valuable genus. The same remarks apply to it as to Chamaecyparis lawsoniana; like them, Thuja species have aromatic foliage. There are many small and medium-sized cultivars.		

SHRUBS

Except where otherwise stated, all the following shrubs will grow in any fertile, well-drained soil. (For *Azalea* see *Rhododendron*.)

*=evergreen	Flowers: season/color	Soil, situation and size	Out-of-flower qualities
Acer japonicum 'Aconitifolium' (A)	Small red flowers in clusters. Midspring.	Moist soil and shelter from wind. Medium.	Deeply lobed leaves turning to a full ruby red in autumn.
A. palmatum (A)	There are many forms and varieties of the Japanese Maple, from small trees to dwarf shrubs. All are worth growing for their delicate, often deeply lobed foliage, which turns to bright colors of gold or red in autumn in almost all of them. Too many of the slow-growing, bushy forms in a garden become oppressive and distracting. The following represent the best varieties for all-seasons purposes.		
A.p. 'Atropurpureum' (A)		Moist soil and shelter from wind. Not a good plant on dry or alkaline soils. Large.	Leaves are a rich purple-maroon from spring to summer, turning vivid red in autumn.
A.p. 'Dissectum Atropurpureum' (A)		As above. Small.	As above, but the leaves are deeply and finely cut. Very dense shrub.
A.p. 'Senkaki' (A)		As above.	Leaves turn light yellow in autumn. All the younger branches are bright coral-red, showing up well in winter. Pruning hard to produce new red shoots is harmful.
Aesculus parviflora (A)	White with red anthers in summer.	Sun or light shade. Medium to large.	Beautiful 'bottlebrush' flowers. Attractive, clear yellow autumn color.
Aronia arbutifolia (A)	White. Spring.	Not on alkaline soil. Sun. Small/medium.	Bright red fruits in autumn and late summer. Brilliant red autumn foliage.
Berberis	This is a very large genus indeed with both evergreen and deciduous members. The former often take on red tints through the winter, while the latter can color well before leaf fall. Almost all have yellow or sometimes orange flowers and blue, red or black berries. *B. darwinii* (E) finds almost universal favor, and makes an excellent hedge.		
Buddleia alternifolia (A)	Midsummer. Lilac, scented.	Full sun. Medium/large.	Few shrubs have such a graceful form, with long curving branches. The flowers appear all along the branches.
Callicarpa bodinieri giraldii (A)	Lilac. Late summer.	Sun or part shade. Medium.	Fruits of a unique shade in plants – a lilac-violet that is almost metallic – and they persist until hit by a hard freeze. Said to be more prolific if grown in a group but experience does not bear this out. Fine autumn color.
Callistemon spp. (E)	Red or yellow (violet in one species) bottlebrushes. Midsummer.	Sun. Small/medium.	All very distinctive plants and they enhance the winter garden with their linear foliage, which is elegantly displayed.

*=evergreen	Flowers: season/color	Soil, situation and size	Out-of-flower qualities
*Calluna vulgaris (A)	The late summer and autumn flowering heathers are discussed on p. 89. There are hundreds of varieties, and a choice should be made from a good catalog, preferably with the advice of a specialist nurseryman who can advise on flower and foliage color and their blending.		
*Camellia (B)	The same considerations apply to Camellia. The genus is discussed on p. 48. A specialist nurseryman will be able to suggest varieties that flower early, late, or midseason and, most importantly, those that are the best ones to grow in your particular climate and conditions. The number of cultivars is so great that it would be of no value to give even a representative selection here and readers should be guided by their own tastes.		
*Carpenteria californica (E)	Large, white. Midsummer.	Full sun and is best against a wall. Medium.	Evergreen foliage against a wall is always an asset.
Caryopteris × clandonensis (A/B)	Blue. Late summer.	Good in alkaline soil. Full sun. Small.	Aromatic foliage. Cut back every other spring.
*Cassinia fulvida (E)	Small white flowers in dense heads. Midsummer.	Full sun. Small.	Golden foliage giving year-round heathlike effect.
*Ceanothus arboreus 'Trewithen Blue' (E)	Spring. Blue.	Not on shallow limestone, but otherwise lime-tolerant. Full sun. Large.	Attractive evergreen foliage.
*C.a. 'Autumnal Blue' (E)	Late summer and autumn. Dark blue.	As above. Medium.	Grown mainly for late blue color but foliage is good. Hardier than most.
*C. 'Cascade' (E)	Spring. Blue.	As above.	Light, airy habit, with neat foliage.
*C. impressus (E)	Midspring. Dark blue.	As above.	Tiny leaves in dense masses, each deeply indented with veins.
*C. papillosus (E)	Late spring. Gentian blue.	As above.	Leaves are unique in the genus and are studded with tiny, sticky glands.
*C. thyrsiflorus repens (E)	Early summer. Light blue.	As above. Small.	Mound-forming habit, excellent for rounded, hummock shape at the front of a border.
*C. × veitchianus (C)	Late spring/early summer. Deep blue, very floriferous.	As above. Large.	Hardier than most others in the genus. Needs more moisture than most and does not do well near a wall.
Ceratostigma willmottianum (B)	Blue. Midsummer to autumn.	Full sun. Good on dry banks. Small.	Reddening foliage in autumn.
Chaenomeles japonica (A)	Late spring/early summer. Orange-red, abundant flowers.	Full sun. Small to dwarf.	Fruits are like small apples, yellow and red, and fragrant. They make good jelly.
C. speciosa (A)	Early spring to early summer. Many vars. with red, pink or white flowers.	Full sun, preferably against a sunny wall. Medium.	Fruits are fairly large, green-yellow with speckles. Plant has a spreading habit.
C. × superba (A)	Red, orange-red or pink. Spring to early summer.	As above. Small to medium.	Small fruits that are light yellow or sometimes red on the sunny side.
Chimonanthus praecox (A)	Winter. Pale yellow with purple center.	Good on alkaline soil. Sun or part shade. Large.	Grown for winter flowers only. Flowers often frozen by sudden drop in temperature.

SHRUBS

*=evergreen	Flowers: season/color	Soil, situation and size	Out-of-flower qualities
*Choisya ternata (E)	Late spring and early summer. Occasionally flowers at other times. Fragrant.	Sun or dappled shade. Medium.	Shining dark green, aromatic foliage of very pleasant appearance.
*Cistus (E)	There are many species, hybrids and cultivars of Cistus with flowers ranging from purple-pink through clear pink to white. Sizes range from small to dwarf. All are excellent on dry banks and in sunny places where they can be mass planted to great effect. Flowering lasts for a long period in summer and their foliage is very handsome, usually in some shade of gray-green. They grow on all soils and are very wind-tolerant, succeeding in maritime exposures. Cistus are less hardy in inland situations than they are in coastal areas.		
*Colletia armata (A/B)	White-flushed, roselike small flower in dense heads. Late summer and autumn. Scented.	Full sun or dappled shade. Large.	Remarkably spiny, dense foliage and rigid habit. Not seen as a hedge but would make a most effective one.
*C. cruciata (E)	White, lightly scented. Late summer and early autumn.	Sun or dappled shade. Slow-growing but eventually fairly large.	Even more formidable, with large, flattened spines.
*Convolvulus cneorum (A)	Large, white flowers. When happy, the plant flowers almost all year round. Main flush of flowers is in late spring/early summer.	Full sun. Dwarf.	Leaves are so well furnished with silky hairs as to appear silver-plated.
Cornus alba 'Sibirica' (A)	Flowers are insignificant.	Damp soil. Small.	Stems are bright red in winter; cut back every other year to produce new, brightly colored stems.
C.a. 'Spaethii' (A)	As above.	Sunny position. Small/medium.	Brilliant yellow variegation of leaves, unfading in sun; bright red stems in winter; cut back as above.
C. mas (A+)	Yellow. Early spring.	Sun. Large.	One of the first shrubs to bloom in spring.
C. stolonifera 'Flaviramea' (A)	Flowers are insignificant.	Sun or part shade. Medium/large.	Stems are bright yellow – highly effective in winter.
*Coronilla glauca (C/D)	Yellow pealike flowers all year round. Main flush in mid-spring. Scented by day.	Sun and shelter from the wind, especially in winter. Small.	Lovely fresh green pinnate foliage with a slight bloom.
Corylopsis pauciflora (A)	Early spring. Yellow catkins appear before the leaves. Scented.	Sun or part shade. Lime hater. Small to medium.	Young, pink leaves appear after flowers.
C. sinensis (A)	Lemon-yellow catkins. Early to midspring. Flowers before leaves.	Sun or part shade. Lime tolerant. Large; sometimes to small tree size.	Ideal host for summer-flowering clematis.
C. willmottiae (A)	Large racemes of soft yellow flowers appear before the leaves. Early spring.	Sun or part shade. Lime tolerant. Large.	Leaves are red-purple when young and they appear after flowering. A good host for later-flowering clematis.
Cotinus coggygria (A)	Inflorescences are tan colored, becoming smoke-gray.	Sun. Large.	Inflorescences are showy for a long time in summer. Good autumn color.

*= evergreen	Flowers: season/color	Soil, situation and size	Out-of-flower qualities
Cotinus coggygria 'Flame' (A)	Inflorescences are tan colored, becoming smoke-gray.	Sun. Large.	Best variety for autumn color; bright orange-red.
C.c. 'Purpureus' (A)	As above.	As above.	Deep brown-purple foliage but not a free-flowering plant.
Cotoneaster	A large genus of very hardy shrubs that will grow almost anywhere; they are discussed on p. 116. The evergreen species are perhaps best for year-round value, but the deciduous species have bright autumn color. All have white or pink flowers in early summer and conspicuous long-lasting, richly hued berries in autumn and winter.		
Cytisus battandieri (B)	Dense heads of yellow flowers (pineapple-scented). Midsummer.	Not on limestone. Best on a wall. except in mild areas. Large.	Shinily silver-plated foliage is evergreen in mild areas and mild winters, otherwise excellent from spring to late autumn.
Daphne	Any daphne is an adornment in a garden and their scent cannot be surpassed. The evergreen species are all possessed of an aristocratic air throughout the year and many deciduous ones are too good to omit. All members succeed in loamy soils with good drainage and their main enemy is drought.		
Desfontainea spinosa (E)	Scarlet, tubular. Late summer.	Lime-free soil. Part shade. Small.	Small, hollylike leaves.
Elaeagnus pungens 'Maculata' (A)	Autumn. Scented but insignificant.	Sheltered location. Medium.	Evergreen leaves, brilliantly variegated with gold. It can be used to great effect in dark corners.
Enkianthus campanulatus (A)	Cup-shaped, rich bronze and yellow. Midspring.	Acidic soil. Dappled shade. Medium.	A great treasure with fine form and among the best of all shrubs for autumn color.
Erica	This very large genus is discussed on pp. 45-46 and p. 72. For all-year round effect it is of the first importance, particularly for those who garden on lime-free soils (although *E. carnea* is lime-tolerant). In protected sites, a long succession of flowering is possible.		
Escallonia (E)	Another large genus of shrubs, valuable for their late flowering and for their glossy evergreen foliage. Flowers range from red to pink with white species and varieties and they make fine evergreen flowering hedges. Escallonias tend to be hardier near the sea.		
Eucryphia × intermedia 'Rostrevor' (E)	Large, white and fragrant flowers. Late summer/early autumn.	Lime-free soil and shelter. Large. They grow best if their roots are shaded.	Beautiful foliage; some leaves simple and some pinnate. Neat, columnar form.
E. lucida (E)	Large, white and scented. Mid- to late summer.	Lime-free soil and shelter. Medium.	Leaves are all simple, small and oblong, giving an impression of great delicacy and elegance.
E. × nymansensis 'Nymansay' (E)	Very large, white. Late summer/early autumn.	Lime-tolerant. Protect from frosty winds. Large.	Larger foliage, both simple and compound, gray-green. Tall columnar form.
Euonymus alatus (A)		Good on any soil. Sun. Large.	Fruits open to show bright scarlet seeds. One of the best shrubs for red autumn color. Twigs have winged outgrowths.
E. oxyphyllus (A)		As above.	Crimson seed capsules open to display scarlet seeds. Autumn color is red and purple.
Fatsia japonica (C)	White. Early autumn.	Part shade and wind-shelter. Much hardier than supposed. Medium.	The largest leaves of any hardy evergreen; palmate on long stems. Gives a subtropical effect.

SHRUBS

* = evergreen	Flowers: season/color	Soil, situation and size	Out-of-flower qualities
Fatsia japonica 'Variegata' (B)	White. Early autumn.	Part shade and wind-shelter. Medium.	Leaves boldly edged with white.
Fothergilla gardenii 'Blue Mist' Mist' (A)	White, 'bottle-brush' flowers. Early spring.	Acidic. Sun or light shade. Dwarf.	Striking blue-green leaves turn orange-red in autumn. Very refined in the small garden.
F. major (A)	Heads of white flowers like bottlebrushes before leaves. Fragrant. Spring.	Lime-free soil. Part shade among other shrubs. Small.	Brilliant autumn colors; gold, orange or red depending on soil and season.
Franklinia alatamaha (A)	White with golden stamens. Fragrant. Late summer.	Rich, acidic, well-drained soil. Light shade. Large.	Red autumn color.
Fuchsia magellanica (B)	Scarlet and violet. Summer and autumn.	Sun or part shade. Small.	Fresh green foliage from spring to autumn. Very long flowering season. Recovers quickly from frosts.
Hamamelis × intermedia 'Arnold Promise' (A)	Primrose-yellow, large, scented and prolific. Late winter.	Sun or part shade. Large.	Orange-yellow autumn color.
H. × i. 'Carmine Red' (A)	Bronze-carmine, strongly scented flowers. Late winter/ early spring.	As above.	Bright gold autumn color.
H. mollis (A)	Yellow. Strongly scented. Late winter/early spring.	As above.	Soft, broad leaves turning gold in autumn.
H. virginia (A)	Yellow. Fragrant. Autumn.	Sun, light shade. Large.	Last shrub to flower each year. Yellow autumn foliage.
Hibiscus syriacus 'Diana' (A)	White. Prolific. Late summer/ early autumn.	Full sun. Medium.	Because this cultivar is a sterile triploid, it does not produce unwanted volunteer seedlings.
Hydrangea	The mopheaded and lacecap hydrangeas are discussed on pp. 81-83. All commercially available varieties are good and it is a matter of choosing for color and for size. *H. quercifolia* (A) has large, white, lacy flowers in early summer, and needs acid soil in full sun or light shade. Its beautiful bold 'oakleaf' foliage turns purple in autumn.		
Hypericum 'Hidcote' (A)	Large, yellow, saucer-shaped. Midsummer to autumn.	Any non-alkaline soil. Full sun, or part shade. Medium.	Grown mainly for the masses of late-borne flowers, but foliage is also good.
Ilex verticillata (A)	Small. Late spring.	Acidic soil. Sun or light shade. Large.	Persistent red fruits and yellow foliage tinged with red, in autumn.
Kalmia latifolia (A+)	Pink to white. Late spring.	Well-drained, acid soil. Sun or light shade. Medium.	Lustrous evergreen foliage. Picturesque form at maturity.
Lavandula stoechas (B)	Deep purple. Summer.	Hot, dry spot. Small.	Leaves are blue-gray, very aromatic.
Leucothöe fontanesiana 'Rainbow' (A)	White, hanging along the branches. Midspring	Acid soil in part shade and moisture. Small.	Gracefully arching stems. Foliage is variegated with pink and cream.
Ligustrum lucidum 'Excelsum Superbum' (B)	Erect panicles of white flowers. Late summer.	Full sun or dappled shade. Large to very large.	Very fine, irregular variegation in cream and yellow.
Lonicera fragrantissima (A)	Cream. Highly scented. Late winter/early spring.	Any soil. Large.	Red berries in midspring.

* = evergreen	Flowers: season/color	Soil, situation and size	Out-of-flower qualities
*Lonicera nitida 'Baggesons Gold' (A)	Insignificant.	Grows anywhere but flower color better in the sun. Medium.	Dense foliage. Leaves are bright gold all year. Takes clipping well.
Magnolia × loebneri 'Leonard Messel' (A)	Pink, star-shaped, fragrant. Midspring.	Large.	Superb tracery of branches in winter with masses of conspicuous, silvery buds.
M. × l. 'Merrill' (A)	Large, white and star-shaped. Fragrant. Midspring.	As above.	As above.
M. sieboldii (A)	White, pendent and fragrant. Flowers on and off from late spring to late summer.	Acidic soil. Part shade. Large.	Grown for its flowers, but it also has a pleasing habit.
M. stellata (A)	White, star-shaped. Mid-spring.	Moist, well-drained soil. Part shade.	Silvery winter buds in profusion even on very young plants.
M. virginiana (A)	White, fragrant. Early summer.	Acidic. Tolerates wet soil. Large.	Dark green leaves with silvery underside. Red-orange conelike fruits in late summer.
*Mahonia aquifolium (A+)	Dense clusters of deep yellow, scented flowers. Late winter to early spring.	Sun or dappled shade. Small.	Glossy blue-green foliage, sometimes red in winter. Decorative fruits, black with blue bloom.
M. bealii (A)	Upright racemes of yellow, scented flowers. Late winter to early spring.	Dappled shade. Medium.	Spiny foliage, broad leathery leaflets.
*M. japonica (B)	Pendulous racemes of yellow, scented flowers. Early winter to early spring.	Sun or dappled shade. Medium.	Magnificent, horizontally held, pinnate, spiny foliage.
*M. lomariifolia (C)	Erect racemes of deep yellow, scented flowers. Winter.	As above, but protect from wind.	Foliage more finely pinnate and even longer. A more elegant plant.
*M. × media (C)	This name covers a race of hybrids between the two previously cited species. Among them are 'Charity', 'Winter Sun', 'Buckland' and 'Lionel Fortescue'. Several are now becoming more widely available and they appear to be very nearly fully hardy. 'Charity' is leggy until cut down once.		
*Mitraria coccinea (E)	Tubular, bright orange-scarlet. All summer.	Not on limestone. Shade and moisture. Small (medium when climbing).	A charming evergreen that makes low, spreading hummocks. It will climb if it meets a suitable tree with fissured bark.
*Myrtus apiculata (E)	White. Late summer, early autumn.	Sun or part shade. Very slow growing, but eventually very large.	Stands severe frost but not with strong winds and not when young. Beautiful black-green foliage and dark purple berries. The bark is spectacular – cinnamon-orange and peeling to show a creamier color beneath.
*Olearia macrodonta (E)	White daisylike flowers. Fragrant. Early summer.	Full sun. It is wind and salt resistant. Medium.	Gray-green, hollylike, evergreen, aromatic foliage.
*O. × scilloniensis (E)	Bush covers itself with white daisylike flowers. Late spring.	Full sun. Small.	Gray-green foliage. Stands severe frost but not with strong wind.

SHRUBS

* = evergreen	Flowers: season/color	Soil, situation and size	Out-of-flower qualities
*Osmanthus × burkwoodii (B)	White and highly scented. Midspring.	Dappled shade. Medium.	Very pleasant, neat, toothed leaves. (BOTANICAL NOTE. Will be found listed as × Osmarea 'Burkwoodii'. As one of its parents has been reclassified from Phillyrea to Osmanthus it is now seen as an Osmanthus × Osmanthus hybrid.)
*O. delavayi (B)	White and jasminelike in appearance. Scented. Midspring.	Full sun or dappled shade. Small.	Neat, rounded leaves.
Parrotia persica (A)	Flowers consist of clusters of crimson stamens all along the branches. Early spring.	Large shrub to small tree.	Brilliant crimson and gold autumn foliage color. Old plants have flaking bark. Horizontal habit brings color and flowers to ground level.
*Pernettya mucronata (E)	White, heathlike. Late spring/ early summer.	Lime-free soil. Part shade. Small.	Dense branches of berries like marbles, persisting well into winter. Varieties (berry color): 'Alba' (white); 'Atrococcinea' (dark red); 'Bells Seedling' (dark red, hermaphrodite form). 'Thymaefolia' is a male form which should be planted with the others to ensure berrying.
Philadelphus coronarius 'Aureus' (A)	White, scented. Midsummer.	Full sun. Medium.	Light gold foliage. Particularly suited for difficult, dry soils.
*Phormium (E)	The phormiums are neither shrubs nor herbaceous plants but are clump forming evergreens with great architectural value. P. tenax has gray-green, sword-like leaves up to 1.8m/6ft tall. There are several varieties, many of which are variegated, some of which are fairly new. Their main use is for outstanding effect in the garden in winter in milder areas. They are not particular about soil but they enjoy sun or a little shade.		
*Photinia × fraseri 'Red Robin' (B)	White. Spring (but only in a sunny climate).	Lime-tolerant. Medium/large.	Large, glossy green leaves. The young growths are brilliant red and the color persists.
*Pieris 'Forest Flame' (A)	White, like Lily of the Valley. Midspring.	Acidic soil. Part shade. Medium.	Panicles of buds form in autumn. New growths brilliant red, becoming pink, then white, and finally green.
*Pittosporum tenuifolium (E)	Chocolate-black but deep wine-ruby against the sun. Late spring.	Wind shelter. Medium/large.	Distinctive, apple-green, undulate foliage, much used in flower arrangement. Will stand hard frost if out of the wind.
*P.t. 'Garnettii' (E)	As above.	As above. Medium.	Gray foliage, margins cream, becoming suffused with pink.
*P.t. 'Abbotsbury Gold' (E)	As above.	As above.	Foliage is yellow-green, variegated with gold.
*Pyracantha coccinea 'Lalandei' (A)	White, massed flowers. Early summer.	Protect from winter winds.	Brilliant red berries covering the shrub from autumn until midwinter.
*P. 'Orange Glow' (A)	As above.	As above.	Orange berries, coloring in late summer while still small, and remaining until spring.
*Rhamnus alaterna 'Argenteovariegata' (B/C)		Will take heavy shade. Medium.	Foliage is variegated in cream and gray. Loved by flower-arrangers and useful for difficult, shady places.

* = evergreen

*Rhododendron

Only a few general guidelines can be given for this huge genus. It is better to grow the species or the species hybrids for all-seasons appeal than it is to choose highly developed plants such as the 'Hardy Hybrids'.

For bark: RR. *barbatum* (large, A/B), *triflorum* (medium, A), *thomsonii* (medium, A), 'Cornish Cross' (large, B/C).

For foliage: RR. *falconeri* (large, A/B), *sinograde* (large, B/C), *macabeanum* (large, B/C), *arizelum* (large, B/C), *calophytum* (large, B/C), *campylocarpum* (small/medium, B/C), *eximium* (large, A/B), *fictolacteum* (large, A), *fulvum* (large, A), *prunifolium* (medium, A), *thomsonii* (medium, A), *williamsianum* and its hybrids (small, A).

For late flowers: RR. *serotinum* (large, A), *griersonianum* and its hybrids (medium, B/C), *auriculatum* (large, A), 'Polar Bear' (large, A), *discolor* (large, A).

For scent: RR. *serotinum* (large, A), *decorum* (large, B/C), *fortunei* (large, A), *auriculatum* (large, A), *discolor* (large, A), 'Albatross' (large, B/C), 'Fragrantissimum' (medium, E), 'Lady Alice FitzWilliam' (medium, D), Loderi and cultivars (B/C), 'Polar Bear' (large, A).

For early flowers: RR. *arboreum* (very large, C/D), *dauricum* (small, A), *mucronulatum* (small, A), 'Praecox' (small/medium, A), 'Emasculum' (small/medium, A).

(*Azalea*)

All azaleas are rhododendrons.
All the deciduous azaleas (which are medium, A) are good for flower in midspring and autumn color. The added bonus of powerful scent is given by *R. luteum* (also known as *Azalea pontica*), which has yellow flowers. Other species: *R. albrechtii* (flowers large, deep rose, autumn color yellow), *pentaphyllum* (flowers early, peach-pink, autumn color orange and red), *schlippenbachii* (flowers large, pink or white, leaves purple at first, orange/red later).
The evergreen (Japanese) azaleas (which are small, A) are good for mass planting. The most common mistake in mass planting is to group them in ones and twos of the same color instead of in blocks.

Rosa

In addition to the groups of old-fashioned roses mentioned on pp. 76-77, the repeat-flowering Bourbons and Hybrid Perpetuals may be included. They require harder pruning than the others but otherwise their cultivation and use is the same. All these roses are hardy. Generally, they make bushes of some 1.5m/5ft high by 90cm/36in wide, although their sizes will, to some extent, be modified by pruning. A selection of roses (excluding species) might consist of the following:-

---

Gallicas

'Assemblage des Beautés' (carmine), 'Belle de Crécy' (pink, changing to parma violet), 'Camaieux' (striped, white crimson and pink, becoming lilac and gray), 'Charles de Mills' (maroon, crimson to lilac and gray), 'Jenny Duval' (lilac, cerise and white), 'Président de Sèze' (deep crimson) and 'Tuscany Superb' (deepest maroon). All are highly scented.

Damasks

'Ispahan' (pink, long-flowering), 'Mme. Hardy' (white), 'Rose de Resht' (bright red, long-flowering), 'York and Lancaster' (white, pink, or pink-and-white, all on the same shrub). All are scented.

Albas

'Félicité Parmentier' (pink at first, then pink-and-cream), 'Koenigin van Dänemarck' (pink), 'Mme. Legras de St. Germain' (white), 'Maiden's Blush' (blush pink) and 'Alba Maxima' (white). All are highly fragrant.

Mosses

'Blanche Moreau' (white), 'Common Moss' (pink), 'Gloire des Mousseux' (deep pink), 'Jeanne de Montfort' (pink with golden stamens), 'Louis Gimard' (very deep lilac-purple), 'Nuits de Young' (very dark maroon) and 'William Lobb' (purple-crimson). All are extremely fragrant.

Bourbons

'Commandant Beaurepaire' (crimson, striped with pink and carmine), 'Honorine de Brabant' (striped pink, lilac and crimson), 'La Reine Victoria' (pink), 'Louise Odier' (pink), 'Mme. Isaac Pereire' (deep rose), 'Mme. Pierre Oger' (silver-pink), 'Souvenir de la Malmaison' (pale pink) and 'Variegata di Bologna' (white, striped with crimson). All are strongly scented.

Hybrid Perpetuals

'Baron Giraud de l'Ain' (crimson, a white line round the deckled edge of each petal), 'Baroness Rothschild' (pale pink), 'Ferdinand Pichard' (striped red and white), 'Prince Camille de Rohan' (deep velvety crimson) and 'Reine des Violettes' (red, changing to purple and gray). All are scented.

SHRUBS

*=evergreen	Flowers: season/color	Soil, situation and size	Out-of-flower qualities
Rhus typhina 'Laciniata' (A+)	Green spikes. Late spring.	Tolerant of hot, dry sites. Large.	Crimson fruit spikes in late summer through winter. Finely cut leaves produce brilliant red autumn color.
Salix irrorata (A)	Catkins in spring before the leaves.	Moist soil, sun or part shade. Not on lime if dry. Medium.	Long shoots, green at first but becoming purple and bloomy.
Sarcococca hookerana (A)	White, very highly scented flowers in late winter/early spring.	Small shrub. Winter shade necessary. All soils, especially limestone.	Winter flowers. Black fruits in autumn.
S. humilis (A)	As above.	As above. Dwarf.	Perfect dwarf, scented, winter-flowering shrub for the very small garden. Fruits black.
Skimmia japonica 'Foremannii' (A)	White and fragrant. Mid-spring.	Winter shade needed. Small.	Aromatic foliage. Bright red, long-lasting berries. Dense, compact habit. Female.
S.j. 'Rubella' (A)	Heads of red buds all winter, then white flowers in mid-spring.	As above.	Dense habit. Male form, ensures berries on 'Foremannii'.
Viburnum betulifolium (A)	White, midsummer.	Sun. Large.	One of the best of all berrying shrubs. Huge clusters of bright red fruits that last right through the winter. Plant more than one for cross-pollination.
V. × bodnantense 'Dawn' (A)	Pink and highly scented. Late autumn and winter.	Sun. Medium.	Grown for winter flowering.
V. × b. 'Deben' (A)	Buds pink, flowers white and highly scented. Late autumn/winter.	As above.	Longer flowering than 'Dawn', lasting until mid-spring.
V. carlesii (A)	Pink in bud, flowers white and very fragrant. Midspring.	Sun or part shade. Medium.	Gray, downy leaves. Good purple-red autumn color.
V. dilatum (A)	Creamy white clusters. Late spring.	Sun or shade. Medium.	Beautiful scarlet fruits in autumn persisting until winter.
V. farreri (A)	Pink in bud, flowers white and very fragrant. Late autumn and all winter.	Sun. Medium.	Grown for its winter flowers and scent. Red fruits are produced in warm climates only.
V. plicatum var. *tomentosum* 'Mariesii' (A)	White. Late spring/early summer.	Sun or part shade. Medium.	Tabular arrangement of branches. Its form is good in winter. Fine red fruits in summer.
Yucca filamentosa (C)	Erect panicles, 1-1.8m/3-6ft tall. White flowers. Early summer.	Sun and good drainage. Small/medium.	Swordlike leaves with curly threads on margins give subtropical effect all year round.
Y. gloriosa 'Variegata' (B)	Erect panicles, 1-1.8m/3-6ft high. Cream flowers. End of summer.	Sun and good drainage. Plant away from paths (spine-tipped leaves).	Species with well-defined trunk and dense heads of sword-shaped leaves, margined cream and yellow. Not usually badly affected by snow unless the plant is covered by drifts, when damage will occur.

CLIMBERS

Climbing plants are not, in the main, plants with all-seasons appeal. Their use is in enhancing the value of other plants upon which they may grow and flowering at times when their hosts are out of flower. One or two, however, are exceptions and do have extra qualities.

* = evergreen	Flowers: season/color	Height and conditions	Extra all-seasons qualities
Actinidia kolomikta (A)	White, fragrant flowers. Mid-summer.	4.5-5.5m/15-18ft. Wall in full sun.	Three-colored variegation – green, white and pink.
Akebia quinata (A)	Red-purple, small and fragrant. Early/midspring.	Up to 9m/30ft. Extremely rampant. Wall or tree.	Unique, steel-blue, sausage-shaped seed pods, 10cm/4in or more long.
Aristolochia macrophylla (A)	Siphon-shaped, yellow and purple. Midsummer.	7.5m/25ft into a suitable tree. Sun or shade.	
*Berberidopsis corallina (E)	Clusters of deep red flowers on long stalks of same color. Late summer.	4.5m/15ft into a large shrub in mild areas. Shade and moist, lime-free soil. In colder areas, needs protection.	Heart-shaped, evergreen leaves.
Campsis radicans (A)	Trumpet-shaped, 7.5-10cm/3-4in long, brilliant orange-red. Late summer.	Up to 15m/50ft. Sunny walls.	
Clematis alpina (A)	Blue and white. Late spring.	1.8-2.5m/6-8ft into a shrub. Sun or shade.	
C.a. 'Frances Rivis' (A)	Larger flowers. Late spring.	To about 3m/10ft in sun or shade.	
*C. armandii (C)	Cream and scented. Late spring.	To about 3m/10ft. Sunny wall. Evergreen.	Leaves are shiny and divided into three leaflets.
C.a. 'Apple Blossom' (C)	Cream and scented, noticeably pink-shaded. Late spring.	As above.	As above.
C. macropetala (A)	Violet, blue center. Late spring/early summer.	To 3m/10ft up a wall or fence or into large shrub.	Silky seed heads.
C. montana 'Elizabeth' (A)	Pink, fairly fragrant and large. Midspring.	Up to 6m/20ft. Shady walls, or into trees.	
C.m. var. *rubens* (A)	Rose-pink. Midspring.	As above.	
C.m. 'Tetrarose' (A)	Rosy-lilac and large. Mid-spring.	As above.	
Clematis – large-flowered varieties	These are well-known clematis of gardens and they are available in many forms and colors, all very useful in the all-seasons garden. They are superb for growing into trees, where the sometimes unnecessarily complicated pruning instructions may safely be ignored. Some flower in late spring and early summer, sometimes with another flush in early autumn, while others bloom from late summer well into the autumn. Flowering time should be chosen so that it will occur when the host tree has either finished flowering or has not yet started.		

CLIMBERS

* = evergreen	Flowers: season/color	Height and conditions	Extra all-seasons qualities
*Hedera	The ivies, though they are useful and hardy evergreens, are plants to be used with the utmost care, since many of them can quickly become a nuisance. It is not generally a good idea to allow them to climb into trees as they look very untidy and conceal wounds and other troubles that should be treated. Small-leaved ivies such as 'Goldheart' are attractive on unimportant walls.		
Hydrangea anomala var. petiolaris (A)	Flowers are white, in 'Lacecap' heads in midsummer.	To 15m/50ft or more, clinging to a tree trunk. Grows to tops of shady walls. Shade.	Reliable, self clinging climber for really shady places.
Jasminum nudiflorum (A)	Bright yellow flowers on leafless branches in the depth of winter.	Grows in all conditions. Medium.	Winter flowers. It can be used to hide ugly walls etc., or it will cover banks of the poorest soil.
J. officinale (B)	White, very fragrant. Late summer.	About 6m/20ft into a tree.	
*J. polyanthum (D/E)	White, pink reverse, highly scented. Late spring to late summer.	Up to 6m/20ft. Warm wall, pergola or tree in mild areas only.	
J. × stephanense (A)	Light pink, highly scented. Midsummer.	6m/20ft or more. Suitable for a wall, pergola or tree.	
*Lapageria rosea (C/D)	Very large, bell-shaped, deep rose. All summer and into autumn.	3.6-4.5m/12-15ft. Lime-free, moist soil. Shady wall or tree.	Evergreen, leathery, gray-green leaves.
Lonicera	The twining honeysuckles can be chosen so that their flowering starts early in the year and goes on into the autumn. They all have some of the most wonderful scents in the garden and flowers ranging from yellow through white to red. Their use should be restricted to garden structures, as they are capable of throttling trees and shrubs. Below is a brief selection of species.		
L. periclymenum 'Belgica' (A)	Flowers are red-purple, fading to yellow. Late spring/early summer.		
L. x brownii (A)	Flowers are orange-scarlet. Late spring, flower again in late summer.		
*L. sempervirens (B)	Flowers are orange-scarlet, yellow within. Midsummer.		
L. caprifolium (A)	Flowers are cream. Midsummer.		
*L. hildebrandiana (D/E)	Giant honeysuckle, 6-9m/20-30ft. Flowers highly scented, cream turning yellow, all summer. Large red berries.		
L. 'Dropmore Scarlet' (A)	Flowers are scarlet. Late summer/autumn.		
L. periclymenum 'Serotina' (A)	Flowers are red-purple. Late summer/autumn.		
Mutisia oligodon (A/B)	Heads of pink, gazania like flowers. All summer and into autumn.	Only about 1.5m/5ft. Sunny site growing into a small shrub.	Does not look good in winter, but this is disguised by a suitable host.
*Passiflora caerulea (C)	Large, a mixture of white, purple, and blue. All summer and autumn.	Between 3 to 4.5m/10 to 15ft. Warm, sunny wall in mild areas.	Evergreen in very mild places. It will survive one very severe winter, but not a succession of them.

*=evergreen	Flowers: season/color	Height and conditions	Extra all-seasons qualities
Rosa	There is a very wide selection of climbing and rambling roses available for growing on pergolas, walls, etc. and many can be grown through trees, especially the Wichuriana group of ramblers. The following are all suitable for the purpose and most are hardy. Those with one main flowering bloom in early to midsummer. Repeat-flowering roses will continue into early autumn.		
Albéric Barbier (A)	Creamy white, large, scented. One main flowering flush.		
Albertine (A)	Copper-pink and scented. One flowering flush.		
Bonfire (A)	Small, pink, in clusters. One main flowering, but a long one.		
Easlea's Golden Rambler (A)	Large, yellow, scented. Nonrecurrent, but heavy flowering.		
Seven Sisters Rose (D)	Flowers in clusters, varying in size. Colors are from pink through mauve to purple. Tender.		
R. brunonii (C)	Rampant. Flowers are large, single and white, borne in clusters. Fragrant. Midsummer.		
R. filipes 'Kiftsgate' (A)	Can reach 15m/50ft into a tree. Become covered with white flowers in summer, followed by orange fruits.		
R. laevigata (C/D)	'Cherokee Rose'. Flowers are large, white and fragrant. Fruits are large. Tender.		
R. longicuspis (A)	Very vigorous. Flowers are white in clusters and banana-scented. Fruits are red.		
Schizophragma hydrangeoides (A+)	White. Lacy flat clusters. Late spring.	Up to 12m/40ft. Sun or partial shade. Any soil.	
Solanum crispum 'Glasnevin' (B)	Potatolike flowers, purple with gold centers. Late summer.	5.5m/18ft. Sun or shade.	
S. jasminoides (C/D)	As above, but pale blue. Late summer to autumn.	Up to 6m/20ft. Sun. Shelter.	
Vitis 'Brant' (A)		Up to 6m/20ft. Tree or pergola. All soils in sun.	Sweet, black, scented grapes. Large, lobed leaves that turn to red and purple in autumn.
V. coignetiae (A)		Up to 6m/20ft. Very vigorous grower. Sun or part shade.	Very large leaves are velvety and turn crimson and scarlet in autumn.
Wisteria floribunda 'Macrobotrys' (A)	Racemes up to 90cm/36in long, lilac tinged with blue, scented. Late spring.	Height depends on training and pruning, but up to 9m/30ft into a tree. Pergola or trained on a wall. Sun.	
W. sinensis (A)	Racemes to 30cm/12in long. Deep lilac, scented. Late spring.	Height depends on training and pruning, but up to 9m/30ft into a tree. Pergola or wall, but excellent in a tree. Sun.	

BULBS

With very few exceptions, those plants that grow from a bulb, corm, or tuber are valuable in the garden for their flowers alone. Many have attractive foliage, but it is in evidence for a relatively short time. They cannot be said to be all-seasons plants but they are, nevertheless, extremely useful in helping to create a garden that is colorful at all times of the year. Those listed below are hardy unless otherwise indicated.

* = evergreen	Flowers: season/color	Height when in flower	Culture
Anemone apennina	Sky blue. Midspring.	15cm/6in	Part shade among tall shrubs. Must never dry out. Can be naturalized in grass.
A. blanda	Blue, white or pink. Early spring.	15cm/6in	Full sun, excels on limestone. Part shade in really hot places.
Arum italicum marmoratum (syn. *pictum*)	Spathe yellow and green. Spring.	20cm/8in	Grown for the beautifully marbled leaves which last through the winter. Sun. Needs winter shade.
Chionodoxa luciliae	Bright blue, clusters of about eight flowers. Midspring.	15cm/6in	Open glades among shrubs. Sun.
Colchicum autumnale	Rose-lilac, purple, or white. Some double forms. Early autumn.	7.5cm/3in	Part shade, around the edges of shrub border or round bases of trees.
C. speciosum	Rose-lilac, purple, or white. Autumn.	20cm/8in	As above.
C. hybrids	Hybrids of the above two species, with crosses to other autumn-flowering species have become the most common colchicums of gardens. Good ones among them are: 'Atrorubens', 'Disraeli', 'The Giant' and 'Water Lily'.		
Crocus biflorus	White to lilac. Early spring.	5cm/2in	Sun and good drainage.
C. chrysanthus	Many colors in many varieties. Early spring.	5cm/2in	Sun and good drainage. Excellent in raised beds.
C. imperati	Late winter to early spring; occasionally midwinter. Buff outside, mauve inside.	7.5cm/3in	Vigorous in a dry, sunny position.
C. laevigatus	Lilac, shaded with lavender. Late autumn to late winter.	5cm/2in	Dry spot in full sun.
C. sativus	Variable shades of purple. Early autumn.	7.5cm/3in	Sun and good drainage.
C. sieberi	Mauve, violet or white. All have golden throat. Early spring.	5cm/2in	Vigorous. Sun and good drainage.
C. speciosus	Deep or light blue or white. Late summer to midautumn.	10cm/4in	Can be allowed free rein in mixed borders. Does not object to disturbance. Sun and good drainage.

* = evergreen	Flowers: season/color	Height when in flower	Culture
Crocus susianus	Deep orange. Early spring.	2.5cm/1in	Dwarf, so plant where its brilliant coloring can be seen to advantage.
C. *versicolor*	White, feathered with purple. Mid spring.	5cm/2in	Sun and good drainage.
Cyclamen europaeum	Deep pink, very fragrant. Late summer.	7.5cm/3in	Rich soil and a warm, sunny position at the edge of a border. Needs winter shade and protection.
C. *neapolitanum*	Deep pink or white. Late summer/early autumn.	10cm/4in	Part shade in rich soil among shrubs. Beautifully marked leaves last for nine months. Needs winter shade and protection.
C. *orbiculatum* var. *coum*	Pink to purple-pink, also white. Succeeding forms from midwinter to spring.	5cm/2in	Round the bases of trees, or in part shade at the edge of a border. Needs winter shade and protection.
Erythronium dens-canis	Pink, violet or white, reflexed. Midspring.	15cm/6in	Peaty or leafy soil in part shade among shrubs.
E. *revolutum*	Pink, lavender or almost white, reflexed. Late spring.	12cm/5in	Moist, semishaded position.
E. *tuolumnense*	Golden, reflexed. Midspring.	Up to 30cm/12in	Rich, moist, peaty soil in shade.
Fritillaria meleagris	Pendulous bells, checkered. Lilac, purple, or white. Mid-spring.	30cm/12in	Sun or part shade. Damp, rich soil but not wet.
Galanthus corcyrensis	White and green markings. Early winter.	10cm/4in	Sun.
G. *elwesii*	White and green markings, large. Mid spring.	12cm/5in	Glades among trees and shrubs or edges of shrub borders.
G. *nivalis*	White and green markings. Late winter/early spring.	10cm/4in	Glades among shrubs and trees.
G. *nivalis* (ssp. *reginae-olgae*)	White and green markings. Midautumn.	12cm/5in	Open position, dry in summer.
G. *plicatus*	White and green markings. Early spring.	10cm/4in	Glades among trees and shrubs.
Iris histrioides	Blue. Late winter to early spring.	10cm/4in	Any soil or situation. Protect from slugs and snails.
I. *reticulata*	Light or dark blue, purple-red or white. Late winter.	15cm/6in	Anywhere except for wet, sticky soils.
Leucojum aestivum	White and green markings. Late spring.	60cm/24in	Damp soil, part shade.

* = evergreen	Flowers: season/color	Height when in flower	Culture
L. autumnale	White, pink tinted. Early autumn.	30cm/12in	Warm, sunny spot.
L. vernum	White with green spot. Early spring.	23cm/9in	Moist soil, sun or part shade.
Lilium auratum	Very large, white with yellow or red markings. Late summer.	1.5-1.8m/5-6ft	Plant 15cm/6in deep among shrubs.
L. regale	Very large, white, deep pink flush outside. Scented. Mid/late summer.	1.5-1.8m/5-6ft	As above.
L. regale 'Royal Gold'	Gold, scented. Mid/late summer.	1.5-1.8m/5-6ft	There are many more lilies in cultivation. These three are perhaps the best.
Narcissus	There are far too many varieties to list but the dwarfer varieties and species are superior to the large florist's daffodils and forms can be found to suit all soils and situations. It is difficult to overdo them, in flower beds or as lawn specimens.		
Nerine bowdenii	Crystal pink. All autumn.	Up to 60cm/24in	Warm, sunny spot. Do not disturb once planted. Hardiness E.
Tulipa greigii and its hybrids	Very large, brilliant scarlet to yellow. Mid spring.	30-45cm/12-18in	Broad, glaucous leaves, boldly streaked with purple.
T. kaufmanniana and its hybrids	White or yellow to pink and red. Early to mid spring.	30-38cm/12-15in	Leaves lie flat and are wavy.

FERNS

All the following ferns require a moisture-retentive soil and some degree of shade. Most will thrive in really shaded positions but they will tolerate sun for part of the day.

Athyrium filix-femina (A)	The Lady Fern has airy, pinnate fronds that appear in spring. It likes open, woodland conditions and reaches a height of about 90cm/36in. Good varieties include 'Plumosum' and 'Victoriae'.
Matteuccia struthiopteris (A)	Vase-shaped masses of pinnate fronds of a fresh, light green appear in spring and last through the autumn. An elegant plant, it can grow to about 60-90cm/26-36in in moist soil.
Osmunda regalis (A)	Very large, noble fronds up to 1.2m/4ft long, pinnate. Likes wet acidic soils.
*Phyllitis scolopendrium (A)	The Hart's-Tongue Fern has evergreen, strap-shaped fronds that are of a bright, glossy green that bring freshness to the garden. There are various crested and twisted forms but none is as beautiful in its simplicity as the type, except perhaps for var. undulatum, whose fronds are wavy.
*Polypodium vulgare (A)	This small evergreen fern will grow into colonies and may, in a humid garden, become epiphytic (able to grow on another plant) in the forks of trees, where it creates an exotic effect.

OTHER PLANTS

There are a great many more herbaceous plants that can be used to produce colorful effects. If too many are planted there is a danger of crowding out other plants and ending up with a summer garden. Few have all-seasons qualities and a herbaceous garden is a sorry sight in winter.

*=evergreen	Flowers: season/color	Height and any special conditions	Uses in the all-seasons garden
Acanthus spinosus (E)	Deep blue-purple. Late summer.	1.2m/4ft and sun.	Long flowering period and late. Bold, cut foliage.
Aconitum autumnale (A)	Spikes of violet flowers. Autumn.	1.2m/4ft.	Very late flowering.
A. henryi 'Spark's Variety' (A)	Lilac-blue spikes. Mid- to late summer.	As above.	Long flowering period.
Agapanthus 'Headbourne Hybrids' (E)	Heads of hanging blue, lily-like flowers. Late summer.	60-90cm/24-36in. Best in moist soil in part shade.	Late flowering.
Anemone japonica (hybs) (A)	White, rose-red or pink. Late summer to midautumn.	46-76cm/18-30in. Deep soil. Excellent in shade.	Very long flowering period and late. Good among shrubs.
Aster × frikartii (A)	Light blue daisies from midsummer to autumn.	60-90cm/24-36in. Sun or part shade.	The most elegant of the asters and disease-free. Extremely long-flowering. Treat as herbaceous by cutting to ground level in early spring.
Diascia rigescens (B)	Long spikes of pink flowers from midsummer to autumn.	45cm/18in. Sun.	Five-month flowering season. Subshrub.
Euphorbia griffithii 'Fireglow' (A)	Orange-red bracts in early summer.	60cm/24in.	Emerging shoots are attractive and the plant has freshness and quality after flowering.
Filipendula hexapetala 'Grandiflora' (A)	Wide heads of cream flowers, mid- to late summer. Scented.	76cm/30in. Any rich soil. Sun or light shade.	Ferny foliage and scent.
Geranium (A)	There are several species and varieties of Geranium. (These are hardy plants and are not to be confused with Pelargonium, a genus that includes the 'geraniums' of florists.) They are without exception excellent, long-flowering plants for ground-cover, thriving in sun or light shade, and should be planted in drifts. Bulbs, particularly small daffodils, associate well and intimately with them.		
Hemerocallis (vars.) (A)	Yellows, reds, orange shades to deep mahogany. Vars. flower from midsummer to early autumn.		For bringing lilylike flowers and bold colors to difficult places.
Primula (A)	The 'Candelabra' primulas are of the utmost value among shrubs or in drifts with other lovers of rich, deep or moist soils. Species are: P. pulverulenta (red), P.p. 'Bartley Strain' (light pink), P. bulleyana (yellow), P. aurantiaca (orange) among others. They are spring-flowering. P. florindae and P. sikkimensis are yellow-flowered, waterside plants from another section of the genus.		
Schizostylis coccinea 'Major' (E)	Spikes of large, deep red flowers in late autumn.	60cm/24in. Any good soil and sun.	Grown for its extreme lateness of flowering.

GLOSSARY

A

Acid Term applied to soils which are almost or completely free of lime in the form of calcium salts.

Alkaline Term applied to soils in which lime, in the form of calcium salts, is present in relatively high concentrations.

Annual A plant that germinates, grows, flowers, sets seed and dies within the space of 12 months.

B

Berry A fleshy or pulpy fruit that does not open. Normally several-seeded.

Bloom (1) A flower.
(2) A waxy, powdery deposit on a leaf, stem or flower.

Bole (of a tree) The trunk or main stem.

Bract A modified leaf, occurring at the base of a flower stalk, flower cluster or shoot. Often petallike.

Bulb A modified shoot with a fleshy, disklike stem which bears a rounded mass of leaves above and produces roots below.

Bush A shrub with a low, compact and dense habit.

C

Calyx The outer whorl of the flower, usually green, but sometimes colored – in most cases the same color as the petals.

Catkin (From the Dutch *katteken*, a kitten.) A spike of unisexual flowers with scaly bracts instead of petals. Used loosely to describe appearance, rather than botanical characteristics.

Corm A modified stem, swollen and containing reserve plant material.

Corymb A flat head of stalked flowers ranged at different levels.

Cultivar A *culti*vated *var*iety; a distinct variant of a species, arising and maintained in cultivation. It is, strictly, an assemblage of identical individual plants, all arising from a single original, from which they have been clonally propagated, or from other individuals in the same assemblage. Each individual bears the same cultivar name, which must now be in a vernacular language (i.e. not in Latin). Often used interchangeably with the term 'variety'.

D

Deciduous Having nonpersistent foliage; (of leaves) falling seasonally.

Dissected Divided into several fine segments.

Dormant A condition of inactivity in plants, usually occasioned by low temperatures.

Double A flower in which there are more than the normal numbers of petals.

E

Epiphytic A plant growing upon another but not deriving any nourishment from it. A fern growing on a tree is epiphytic; a climber growing up another plant is not.

Evergreen Retaining foliage in winter.

F

Fastigiate Having branches close together and erect.

Floriferous Capable of reliably bearing large numbers of flowers.

Form (1) A term used to denote the attributes of a plant, other than its flowers, which, taken together, give it its general character and appearance.

(2) A loose term covering 'cultivar', 'variety', and unnamed versions of species.

Frond The leaf of a fern or palm.

Fruit A term used to denote many kinds of ornamental seed vessel, including berries and rose-hips.

G

Genus A group of species with common structural characters.

H

Habit General appearance or manner of growth of a plant, e.g. upright, sprawling, creeping, etc.

Herbaceous Dying down to ground level in winter.

Hybrid A plant that has resulted from the crossing of two or more species. Where two species only are involved, the hybrid may be given its own Latin name, denoted by an ×. E.g. *Camellia × williamsii.*

I L

Inflorescence The flowers of a plant and the flower-stalks.

Lanceolate (of leaves) Lance-shaped.

Leaflet One of the parts of a compound leaf.

Linear (of leaves) Long and narrow, the margins nearly parallel.

M N

Monoculture A system of horticulture where only one crop, or one genus of plants, is grown.

Node A leaf joint, i.e. the place where the leaf joins the stem.

O P

Oblong (of leaves) Almost parallel-sided and longer than broad.

Palmate Lobed so as to appear like a spread hand.

Panicle A branching raceme.

Pinnate Of compound leaves with leaflets arranged on either side of the central stalk.

Perennial Persistent from year to year.

Q R

Quartered (of flat-topped blooms of old-fashioned roses) Having petals packed in whorls, often four in number.

Raceme A simple inflorescence, like a spike, but with stalked flowers.

S

Semievergreen Normally evergreen, but surviving defoliation in cold areas or severe winters.

Shrub A woody plant, branching from the base and with no true trunk.

Spike A simple, elongated inflorescence in which the flowers have no individual stalks.

Species A group of individual plants with constant characteristics that make them appear almost identical, even though, in minute detail, they may not be. A species is a subdivision of a genus.

Stooling The practice of cutting the main stem of a tree to ground level in order to produce many stems bearing, in many cases, juvenile foliage.

T

Tree A woody plant producing a single main trunk and having a more or less elevated head of branches.

Tuber A swollen underground branch, capable of producing shoots and roots.

U V

Undulate With wavy margins.

Variegated Patterned with at least two colors.

Variety (1) (loosely) A cultivar (q.v.) or a true botanical variety (see 2). (2) A group of plants within a species, showing common characteristics that distinguish them from other members of the species. A true botanical variety is found in the wild, and has a Latin varietal name. Abbreviation: var.

INDEX

ACKNOWLEDGMENTS

Publishers' acknowledgments

The publishers would like to thank the following individuals for their help in producing this book: Steven Wooster for initial design, Claudine Meissner, Mark Richards and Judith Robertson for their help with the design and The Hon. Mrs. Lyttelton for allowing her garden to be photographed. Also, thanks go to Joanna Chisholm, Paul Meyer and Hal Bruce for their help with the American edition, to Cathy Gill for the index and to Susan George for clerical help.

Editor Sarah Mitchell
Art editor Bob Gordon
Text editor Jonathan Hilton
Picture researcher Anne Fraser

Typesetting
Chambers Wallace Ltd, London

Reproduction
Universal Colour Scanning Ltd, Hong Kong

Photographers
Heather Angel 117
Tony Bates 20bl, 53t, 56, 75t, 83, 87, 105, 110tm, b
Geoff Dann 6, 19, 20br, 22, 24, 28, 29, 45t, 48, 49, 52, 53bl, 60, 65, 70, 71t, 72, 75b, 76, 77rt, 78, 79, 81, 88, 90, 91, 97b, 100t, 101, 102, 110tl, tr, 115
Inge Espen-Hansen 23, 63, 74, 77l, 100b, 116
Derek Fell 1, 2, 4, 14, 43, 51, 53br, 92, 94, 120t
Jerry Harpur 12, 13, 35, 68, 69, 95, 99, 109
Marijke Heuff (Amsterdam) 25, 26, 27, 32, 33, 47, 82, 96, 103, 112, 113, 118, 119, 120b, front and back cover
Neil Holmes 10, 11, 36, 42
John Glover 34, 89, 104
Georges Lévêque 9, 17, 31, 55, 61, 73
Tania Midgley 71b
David Russell 44, 45b, 57, 66, 97t
Pamla Toler (Impact Photos) 67
Elizabeth Whiting & Associates 20t (Karl Dietrich Bühler), 21 (Neil Lorimer), 62 (Di Lewis)

Illustrators
David Ashby 36, 37, 38
Michael Craig 15, 39, 121, 134
Fiona Curry 64, 66, 86, 98, 114
Andrew Farmer 122-133
Sally Launder 40-1, 58-9, 84-5, 106-7
Josephine Martin (Garden Studio) 18, 50, 108
Jill Ogilvy 80, 111

Cover border illustration
Michael Craig

Garden designers
Ken Akers (Great Saling) 99, 109
Mr & Mrs Cooke 21
Mr & Mrs Bennekom-Scheffer front + back cover, 32, 33, 47, 96, 103, 118, 119
Mr & Mrs Dekker-Fokker 112, 113
Jaap Nieuwenhuis and Paula Thies 120b

Garden plans
Robin Williams 36, 37, 38

KEY
b=bottom; t=top; l=left; r=right; m=middle